# New Ninja Dual Zone Air Fryer Cookbook UK

Simple & Affordable Ninja Foodi Recipes to Fry, Roast, Grill and Bake The Whole Family and Busy People

## Von D. Branan

# Contents

# How the Ninja Dual Zone Airfryer changed my approach to cooking:

I never really enjoyed cooking growing up. It was always a chore that I had to do, and I never really saw the appeal. But when I got my first apartment after college, I realized that I would have to learn how to cook if I wanted to eat anything other than noodles every day.

So, I started doing some research and came across the Ninja Dual Zone Airfryer. It looked perfect for someone like me who didn't know how to cook but wanted to learn. The air fryer has two separate compartments, so you can cook two different things at the same time.

I decided to give it a try, and I'm so glad I did! When I received my Ninja Dual Zone Airfryer, I was a little intimidated by all of the features. However, after reading through the manual and playing around with it a bit, I found that it is actually quite simple to use. I've even found myself enjoying cooking now!

With the airfryer, all you have to do is place your food in the basket, select a Cook Time, and press start. That's it! The machine does all the work for you, ensuring that your food cooks evenly and comes out crispy and delicious every time. Additionally, the airfryer doesn't require any oil, so you can enjoy your favourite fried foods without all the guilt.

I can cook my food in a fraction of the time it used to take me. The Ninja Dual Zone Airfryer is truly a game-changer when it comes to cooking. It has helped me enjoy cooking again by making it simpler and more convenient than ever before. So whether you're an experienced chef or a beginner cook, the Ninja Dual Zone Airfryer is a great option for you.

If you've ever wished you could make all of your favourite fried foods without all the oil and mess, then you need this cookbook!

This cookbook will show you how to make all of your favourites, from chicken tenders to French fries, in this amazing appliance. Not only does the airfryer require little to no oil, but it also cooks food evenly and quickly, meaning you'll never have to worry about undercooked or burnt food again. Whether you're a beginner or a seasoned pro in the kitchen, this cookbook has something for everyone. So what are you waiting for? Get cooking with the Ninja Dual Zone Airfryer today!

## Getting to know the Ninja Dual Zone Airfryer:

The Ninja Dual Zone Airfryer is a unique kitchen appliance that can do more than just fry food. It can also bake, roast, and grill. This all-in-one appliance is perfect for those who want to save time and space in the kitchen.

# So, what exactly can the Ninja Dual Zone Airfryer do?

**Fry**: The airfryer uses super-heated air to fry food without the need for oil. This means that you can enjoy your favourite fried foods without all the unhealthy fat and calories.

**Bake**: The airfryer can also be used to bake cakes, cookies, pies, and other desserts. Just preheat the oven and place your baked goods inside. The airfryer will do the rest!

**Roast**: Love roasted chicken or veggies? The airfryer can do that too! Just place your food in the oven and let it cook until it's nice and crispy.

**Grill**: Craving a juicy burger or steak? Grill it up in the airfryer! You'll get perfectly cooked meat every time.

# Why you should get a Ninja Dual Zone Airfryer today?

If you're looking for an air fryer that can do it all, the Ninja Dual Zone Airfryer is the one for you. Here are four reasons why you should get one today:

1. The <u>Dual Zone</u> feature means you can cook two different foods at once, or cook one food at two different temperatures. This is perfect for those times when you want to cook a quick meal but also need to bake something.

2. The <u>Air Crisp</u> Technology ensures that your food comes out nice and crispy, without the need for oil. So whether you're making French fries or chicken wings, they'll come out perfectly cooked every time.

3. The Ninja Air Fryer is <u>large</u> enough to feed the whole family, but also has a small footprint so it doesn't take up too much counter space.

4. The Ninja Air Fryer is <u>very easy to use</u>, with a simple control panel that makes it easy to set the temperature and timer. Plus, the included cookbook has recipes for everything from breakfast to dessert, so you can make any meal in your air fryer.

### Main Features of the Ninja Dual Zone Airfryer:

The Ninja Dual Zone Airfryer is a unique appliance that allows you to cook two different foods at the same time. It has two independent cooking zones with separate temperature controls. This

means that you can cook two different foods at different temperatures, or even cook one food in each zone simultaneously.

The airfryer also has a built-in fan that circulates hot air around the food, giving it a crispy, fried texture without all the oil. And because it uses less oil than traditional frying methods, it's healthier too!

Here are some of the other features that make the Ninja Dual Zone Airfryer so great:

**1. Large Capacity** – The airfryer can hold up to 4 litres of food, making it perfect for large families or entertaining guests.

**2. Fast Cooking** – The powerful airflow of the airfryer cooks food quickly and evenly, so you can have a delicious meal on the table in no time.

**3. Easy to Use** – The airfryer is simple to operate with one touch controls and an easy-to-read digital display.

**4. Safe** – The airfryer features automatic shut-off and cool-touch housing, making it safe to use in your home kitchen.

**5. Versatile** – The airfryer can be used to cook a variety of foods, from chicken wings to French fries, and everything in between!

# How does it work?

If you're like most people, you probably think of air fryers as nothing more than a trendy kitchen gadget. But the truth is, there's a lot of science behind how they work.

### Here's a quick rundown:

Air fryers use a technique called convection cooking, which means they circulate hot air around food to cook it evenly. They also typically have a built-in fan that helps circulate the air.

Most air fryers have a heating element near the bottom and a fan at the top. As the air fryer heats up, the hot air rises and circulates around the food. This circulating hot air cooks the food quickly and evenly on all sides.

One of the best things about air frying is that you can cook food with little to no oil. This means that you can enjoy your favourite fried foods without all the unhealthy fat and calories. It also means that cleanup is a breeze since there is very little oil to deal with.

So how does this all translate into better-tasting food? In short, it means that your food will be cooked evenly throughout, with no dry spots or overcooked edges. And since air fryers cook so quickly, they can help preserve more of the natural moisture in food, resulting in juicier, tastier results.

# What foods can I cook in the airfryer?

There are a number of different foods that you can cook in an air fryer. Some of the most popular include chicken, fish, and vegetables.

You can also cook frozen foods in an air fryer, such as french fries or chicken nuggets.

When cooking chicken in an air fryer, it is best to use boneless, skinless chicken breasts. Cut the chicken into small pieces so that it cooks evenly. Season the chicken with your favourite spices or marinade before cooking. Cook the chicken for 10-15 minutes at 190 degrees Celsius until it is cooked through.

Fish is another great option for air frying. Cut the fish into small fillets or cubes and season with salt, pepper, and your favourite herbs or spices. Cook the fish for 8-10 minutes at 190 degrees Celsius until it is cooked through.

Vegetables are a healthy option for air frying as well. Cut them into small pieces so they cook evenly. Season with salt, pepper, and your favourite spices before cooking. Cook veggies for 8-10 minutes at 190 degrees Celsius until they are tender but not mushy.

Frozen foods can be cooked in an air fryer as well. No need to thaw them first, just place them in the basket and cook according to the package Directions. French fries typically take 10-15 minutes to cook while chicken nuggets usually take 8-10 minutes

### How to clean the Ninja Dual Zone Airfryer:

If you're like most people, you probably don't think much about cleaning your air fryer. But if you want it to last and continue working well, it's important to clean it regularly. Here's how to clean the Ninja Dual Zone Air Fryer:

- 1. Unplug the air fryer and remove any food or debris from the baskets.
- 2. Wash the baskets with warm, soapy water. Rinse thoroughly and dry with a clean towel.
- 3. Wipe down the outside of the air fryer with a damp cloth. Be sure to wipe away any grease or food splatters.
- 4. When you've finished cleaning the air fryer, make sure all of the parts are dry before reassembling it. Once it's all put back together, your air fryer will be ready to use!
- 5. Once a week, deep clean the air fryer by removing the baskets and heating element. Wash them both with warm, soapy water. Rinse thoroughly and dry completely before putting them back in the air fryer.

# What can go wrong?

When using any kind of cooking appliance, there are always potential risks and wrongdoings that can occur. The Ninja Dual Zone Airfryer is no different.

Here are some possible risks and wrongdoings that could happen when using this airfryer:-

- Using too much oil or fat in the airfryer. This can cause the food to become greasy and unhealthy.
- Not preheating the airfryer before cooking. This can lead to uneven cooking and potentially burnt food.
- Overcrowding the airfryer basket. This will cause the food to not cook evenly and could result in burnt food.
- Not cleaning the airfryer regularly. This can cause a build-up of grease and grime on the appliance, which can be a fire hazard.

### Tips and Tricks

Looking to get the most out of your Ninja Dual Zone Air

Fryer?

Check out these 10 tips and tricks for making the most of this incredible appliance!

1. Preheat your air fryer before cooking. This will help ensure that your food cooks evenly and comes out crispy and delicious.

2. Cut your food into even pieces. This will help ensure that all of your food cooks evenly and gets nice and crispy.

3. Use the dual zone feature to cook different foods at the same time. The dual zone feature allows you to cook two different types of food at the same time, so you can make a complete meal in one go!

4. Experiment with different recipes and seasonings to find your perfect dish!

5. Use an oil sprayer to coat your food with oil. This will help it crisp up nicely in the air fryer.

6. Don't overcrowd your air fryer basket. This will prevent air from circulate properly and can result in uneven cooking.

7. Shake or flip your food halfway through cooking to ensure even results.

8. Use the manual mode if you want more control over the cooking process. The manual mode allows you to set a specific temperature and cooking time.

9. Use tongs or a spatula to flip or remove food from the basket, as opposed to using your fingers. The hot air can be intense!

10. Allow cooked food to rest for a minute or two before serving, as this will help it retain its heat and flavor.

## FAQ's

- *What is the benefit of having two zones?*

  The two zones also allow you to cook different foods at different temperatures, so you can perfectly cook everything from chips to chicken wings. The airfryer is also perfect for cooking frozen food straight from the freezer, as well as fresh food.

- *What are the best foods to cook in the airfryer?*

  Anything that can be cooked in a traditional fryer can be cooked in an air fryer. The main difference is that food cooked in an air fryer will be healthier because it will have less oil. To get the best results, it is important to preheat the air fryer and cook the food in batches.

- *What foods to avoid cooking in the airfryer?*

  Foods with high water content such as soup or stew. Also, breaded foods or those with a high sugar content can cause the food to stick to the basket or burn.

- *Can I use oil in the airfryer?*

  You can use oil in the Ninja Dual Zone Airfryer, but it's not necessary. The air fryer will work without oil, but if you're looking for a bit of extra flavor, you can add a teaspoon or two of your favourite oil to the fryer basket before cooking.

- *Can I put foil in the airfryer?*

  You can put foil in the airfryer, but make sure that it doesn't touch the heating element. If you're using the dual zone function, you can put the foil in the second zone so that it doesn't come into contact with the food.

- *Can I cook raw meat in the Ninja Dual Zone Airfryer?*

  You can cook raw meat in the Ninja Dual Zone Airfryer, but it is important to note that you will need to cook it in the correct way to ensure that it is safe to eat. Always ensure that you cook meat thoroughly, and follow the instructions in the manual carefully.

- ***Do I need to preheat the airfryer?***

  For best results, we recommend preheating the Ninja Dual Zone Airfryer for 3 minutes at 200°C/400°F before adding your food.

- ***Is airfrying healthier than deep-frying?***

  Airfrying is definitely a healthier option than deepfrying. Not only does it use less oil, but the food also retains more of its nutrients.

- ***Can you fill an airfryer basket to the top?***

  No, you should never fill an airfryer basket to the top. The airfryer needs space to circulate hot air, so if the basket is too full, your food will not cook evenly.The Ninja Dual Zone Airfryer has two zones, so you can cook multiple items at once without overcrowding the basket.

- ***Can you open an airfryer while it is cooking?***

  No, you can't open an airfryer while it is cooking. If you need to check on your food, you can pause the cooking timer and then open the airfryer.

# Air fryer breakfast Yorkshire pudding
**HANDS-ON TIME 15 MIN, OVEN TIME AROUND 1 HOUR**
### Serves 1-2

## Ingredients
- 2 pork sausages
- 100g small tomatoes on the vine
- 2 British outdoor-bred streaky bacon slices
- 1 fresh rosemary sprigs, halved

**Batter Ingredients**
- 70g plain flour
- 100ml whole milk

- Olive oil for drizzling
- 1 large portobello mushrooms
- A few sprigs fresh thyme
- 2 medium free-range eggs

- 2 medium free-range eggs, beaten

## Direction
Step 1. To make the batter, whisk the 70g plain flour and beat the 2 eggs in a bowl until smooth.

Step 2. Gently add the 100ml whole milk and whisk until smooth, then season with salt and pepper and set aside.

Step 3. The Ninja Foodi air fryer should be preheated to 200°C/180°C. The sausages should be placed in a roasting pan, sprayed with olive oil, and roasted for 15 minutes to lightly color.

Step 4. Place the mushrooms, tomatoes, and bacon in the tin. Add a little oil from the tin's bottom, along with the thyme and rosemary, and season to taste.

Step 5. The air fryer should be heated to 220°C/200°C. After 10 minutes, place the tin back in the air fryer; after that, remove it and add the batter.

Step 6. Put the tin back into the air fryer and cook it for another 25 to 30 minutes, or until the batter is puffed and golden.

Step 7. Put the pudding back in the air fryer, then crack the remaining eggs into the low sections of the dish, and cook for an additional 6 to 8 minutes, or until the egg whites are set but the yolks are still runny. Serve hot.

# Egg in a Basket
**Prep TIME 1 min / Cook Time / 9 mins / Total Time 10 mins**
### Servings 4

## Ingredients
- 4 slice bread

- 4 egg

## Directions
Step 1. the Air Fryer to 330 degrees before using it. Spray the heated basket with nonstick cooking

spray and place a piece of parchment paper inside.

Step 2. Slice the bread, make a hole in the middle of the loaf. Placing the bread in the Air Fryer basket's basket on the parchment paper.

Step 3. The middle of the slice of bread should now contain the cracked egg.

Step 4. Eggs should be heated in a basket for 5 minutes at 330 degrees while the Air Fryer Basket is closed. After carefully flipping the egg in the hole with a spatula, cook for an additional 3–4 minutes.

Step 5. After removing from the Air Fryer, season with salt and pepper before serving.

## Tortillas

- 395g pack Ground sausage
- 56g Chopped red or gold potatoes
- 42g red, green, and yellow diced bell peppers
- 1/2 tsp salt
- 1/2 tsp garlic powder
- 55g shredded cheese
- 2 tbsp olive oil
- Second protein (ham, ground chicken, bacon)
- 42 g purple (red) onion
- 6-8 eggs
- 1 tsp pepper
- 1 tsp Italian seasoning
- 2 tbsp butter

## Directions

Step 1. Melt 3 tbsp of olive oil and 2 tbsp of butter over medium heat. About 7-8 minutes after adding the potatoes, add the onions and peppers. Sauté for a further 3–4 minutes. Heat has been removed; set aside.Cook the proteins, then drain and set aside.

Step 2. Eggs should be scrambled while being lightly salted and peppered.The eggs should first be placed in the tortilla's middle.

Step 3. Use the back of a spoon to gently press down so that it will contain the remaining Ingredients.

Step 4. Add your proteins, then the potatoes and vegetables that have been sautéed, finishing with cheese.

Step 5. Tightly roll the burrito.Place the filled burritos in the air fryer basket and brush with melted butter or cook with cooking spray. 5 to 6 minutes of air frying at 330 degrees Fahrenheit.

# Breakfast Burrito
### Prep TIME 20 minutes / Cook Time 5 mins / Total Time 35 mins
### Servings 12 tortillas

## Ingredients
**Tortillas**
- 395g pack Ground sausage
- 56g Chopped red or gold potatoes
- 42g red, green, and yellow diced bell peppers
- 1/2 tsp salt
- 1/2 tsp garlic powder
- Second protein (ham, ground chicken, bacon)
- 42 g purple (red) onion
- 6-8 eggs
- 1 tsp pepper
- 1 tsp Italian seasoning

- 55g shredded cheese
- 2 tbsp olive oil
- 2 tbsp butter

## Directions

Step 1. Melt 3 tbsp of olive oil and 2 tbsp of butter over medium heat. About 7-8 minutes after adding the potatoes, add the onions and peppers. Sauté for a further 3–4 minutes. Heat has been removed; set aside.Cook the proteins, then drain and set aside.

Step 2. Eggs should be scrambled while being lightly salted and peppered.The eggs should first be placed in the tortilla's middle.

Step 3. Use the back of a spoon to gently press down so that it will contain the remaining Ingredients.

Step 4. Add your proteins, then the potatoes and vegetables that have been sautéed, finishing with cheese.

Step 5. Tightly roll the burrito.Place the filled burritos in the air fryer basket and brush with melted butter or cook with cooking spray. 5 to 6 minutes of air frying at 330 degrees Fahrenheit.

# Breakfast Pizza

**Prep TIME 5 minutes / Cook Time 15 mins / Total Time 20 mins**
**Servings 4**

## Ingredients

- Crescent Dough
- 1/2 chopped pepper
- 42g cup mozzarella cheese
- crumbled sausage
- 42g cup cheddar cheese

## Directions

Step 1. Drizzle oil to the pan then spread dough in the bottom of the pan. Place in the ninja foodie air fryer on 350 for 5 minutes or until the top is slightly brown. Remove from the air fryer and top sausage, peppers, and cheese Or with your favorite toppings.

Step 2. Place in the air fryer for an additional 5-10 minutes or until the top is golden brown.

# Air fryer breakfast banana bread

**Prep TIME 10 minutes / Cook Time 20 mins / Total Time 30 mins**
**Servings 6**

## Ingredients

- 170g cups of flour
- 1 teaspoon of baking powder
- 1 teaspoon of cinnamon
- 134g cups of sugar
- 3 overripe bananas
- 170g cups of milk
- 1 teaspoon of baking soda
- 1 teaspoon of salt
- 170g cup of oil

## Directions

Step 1. In a mixer or a big mixing bowl, combine each ingredient.After that, apply nonstick cooking spray to coat your pan (or use olive oil)

Step 2. Cook for 20 to 30 minutes at 330 degrees F (air fryer setting). Does the toothpick come out clean when you check your air fryer? If so, it is finished; if not, let yourself a few more minutes.

Step 3. Slice after cooling, then plate.

# Air fryer Monkey Bread

**Prep TIME 10 minutes / Cook Time 20 mins / Total Time 30 mins**
**Servings 6**

## Ingredients

- 12 Any pre-made frozen dough, dough thawed to room temperature
- 110g brown sugar
- 1 teaspoon cinnamon
- 4 tablespoons butter melted

**Glaze**

- 100g powdered sugar
- 1-2 tablespoons milk
- ½ teaspoon vanilla

## Directions

Step 1. In a separate dish, mix the cinnamon and brown sugar. In a another dish, melt one-half of a stick of butter. Melted butter should be lightly brushed throughout an oven-safe pan that may be used for air frying.

Step 2. Once your rolls have thawed to room temperature, divide them in half, roll them in butter, and then dip them in the sugar mixture before putting them on the pan. Repeat!

Step 3. Once all of the rolls are in the pan, add any leftover butter and sugar on top.In an air fryer that has been preheated and turned OFF, rolls should rise for 30 minutes, just to the top of the pan.

Step 4. Rolls should be carefully covered with foil to prevent the top from burning before baking for 10 to 20 minutes at 340 °F/171 °C. When a bread instant-read thermometer registers around 180 °F/82 °C, it is cooked.

Step 5. While baking, prepare the glaze by mixing milk, vanilla, and powdered sugar until it becomes just barely runny.

Step 6. To slightly brown the top, remove the foil and bake for one to three more minutes. Remove pan from oven with care.

Step 7. Just one minute should pass after which you should flip the pan over onto a dish.
Glaze it, then serve and enjoy.

# Baked Apples Air fryer

**Prep :  10 minutes / Cook Time : 15 minutes / Total Time : 25 mins**
**Servings 2**

## Ingredients

- 2 medium apples
- 15 g all-purpose flour
- 28 g unsalted butter or coconut oil
- 3/4 tsp ground cinnamon
- 2 tbsp raisins
- 46 g rolled oats
- 25 g brown sugar or coconut sugar*
- 15 g pecans optional
- pinch of salt

## Directions

Step 1. Apples should be cut in half (through the stem) and the stem and core should be removed. Make sure they are the proper size to fit in your ninja foodi air fryer and, if required, remove more of them.

Step 2. They shouldn't be allowed to touch the upper element some toppings can bubble over, so make any necessary preparations for your ninja foodi air fryer.

Step 3. Set the temperature of your Ninja Foodi air fryer to 325 °F (162 °C). Everything, excluding the apples and raisins, should be combined in a small dish.

Step 4. A spoonful of raisins must be placed in the center of each apple. The raisins should be positioned in between the crumble and the apples to prevent scorching.To prevent the crumble topping from moving around in the air fryer, divide it among the four apple halves and press it firmly over the raisins.Place them in the air fryer very gently, crumble topping side up.

Step 5. Cook until softened for 13–18 minutes. The crumble mixture will have begun to brown, and the apples will have softened but not become mushy. As they sit, they'll soften a little bit more.

# Air fryer Bagel Dogs

**Prep : 5 minutes / Cook Time : 10 minutes / Total Time : 15 mins**
**Servings 2-4**

## Ingredients

- 1 package puff pastry or 1 tube of Crescent Roll dough
**Everything Seasoning:**
- 2 tbsp poppy seeds
- 2 tbsp sesame seeds
- 1 1/2 tsp coarse salt
- 2 tbsp baking soda
- 1 package hot dogs

- 2 tbsp dried minced onion
- 1 1/2 tsp garlic powder
- 680l water

## Directions

Step 1. Set ninja foodi air fryer to 400 degrees Fahrenheit.

Step 2. Ignore the perforated lines when you unfold the dough into a single sheet for Crescent rolls. Or take one sheet of thawed puff pastry from the freezer.

Step 3. Make strips of dough that are one inch thick. Each hot dog is wrapped with one strip.

Step 4. To make the seasoning, mix the salt, sesame seeds, poppy seeds, dried onion, and garlic powder in a small dish. Place aside.

Step 5. Put some water in a small dish. It's warm and a touch steamy after approximately a minute, Add baking soda and whisk to combine.Each dough-wrapped hot dog should be dipped into the baking soda-water solution using tongs, getting it completely saturated.

Step 6. Each dipped dog should be placed onto a air fryer basket lined with paper and generously sprinkled with everything seasoning. Cooking time for hot dogs is 8 to 10 minutes. Serve and enjoy.

# Quiche Air fryer

**Prep : 5 minutes / Cook Time : 15 minutes / Total Time : 20 mins**
**Servings 3**

## Ingredients

- 6 large eggs
- 1 teaspoon kosher salt
- ½ teaspoon black pepper
- 340g whole milk or dairy-free milk
- ½ teaspoon garlic powder

## Directions

Step 1. Two ramekins should be greased with olive oil or nonstick baking spray.

Step 2.Whisk everything together in a big bow then divide the mixture among the ramekins that have been ready. Add any desired toppings. Cook the quiche in the ramekins in the ninja foodi air fryer basket at 350 °F for 16 minutes, or until the center of the quiche is no longer moist. Serve.

# Egg Rolls Air fryer

**Prep : 10 minutes / Cook Time : 8 minutes / Total Time : 20 mins**
**Servings 4**

## Ingredients

- 4 strips bacon
- 2 large eggs
- 4 tbsp vegetable oil
- 1 tsp salt
- 128g cup cooked hashbrowns
- 4 egg roll wrappers
- 43g cheddar cheese
- 1/2 tsp pepper

## Directions

Step 1. One egg roll wrapper need to be placed flat on a table with one corner facing toward the belly button. The proper components should be arranged in a straight line in the center of the egg roll wrapper. It should be about an inch wide, extend the diagonal length of the egg roll wrapper, and leave a 1/2-inch gap at either end.

Step 2. Up until the fold hits the filling's end, the egg roll's two corners should be tucked in.

Step 3. Fold the two tucked-in corners of the egg roll wrapper over first, then the egg roll filling, starting on the other side. The eggroll should be tightly wrapped up into a cylinder (but not too tightly).

Step 4. Apply water to the eggroll's edge using a basting brush to seal it.Spray vegetable oil on the eggroll's outside before cooking it in an air fryer at 375 degrees for 8 minutes, rotating it halfway through.

# Egg pizza Air fryer

**Prep : 5 minutes / Cook Time : 10 minutes / Total Time : 20 mins**
**Servings 2 pizza**

## Ingredients

- 1 English muffin
- 2 eggs
- 32g mini Pepperoni
- OPTIONAL GARNISH - Italian seasoning, red pepper flakes and Parmesan

- 85g pizza sauce
- 43g shredded Mozzarella cheese

## Directions

Step 1. Cut the English muffin in half, then scoop out the middle to create a concave shape.

Step 2. Add two tablespoons of pizza sauce on the top of each piece of bread.Over the bread's middle, crack an egg. Add a dash of salt and pepper on top. Add shredded mozzarella, pepperoni, and a dash of Italian herbs to the egg's top.

Step 3. Add shredded mozzarella, pepperoni, and a dash of Italian herbs to the egg's top.Pizzas should be placed carefully in the NInja Foodi Air Fryer basket and cooked for 8 to 10 minutes at 375°F, or until the egg whites are set.

Step 4. Pizzas should be served with Parmesan and red pepper flakes on top.

# Baked twice potatoes Air fryer

**Prep : 5 minutes / Cook Time : 10 minutes / Total Time : 15 mins**
**Servings 4**

## Ingredients

- 2 cooked baked potatoes
- 43g cheddar cheese
- 2 slices bacon, cooked

- 2 Tablespoon sour cream
- 1 Tablespoon butter

## Directions

Step 1. Scoop the insides of the cooked potatoes into a bowl after cutting them in half.

Step 2. To the bowl of potatoes, add the sour cream, 1/4 cup of cheddar cheese, and the butter.

Step 3. Use a potato masher to combine the Ingredients and mash the potatoes until they are the appropriate consistency.Re-spoon the contents into the potato shells, piling them up as needed to fit.

Step 4. Keep chilled until you're ready to serve.

Step 5. The potatoes should be placed in an air fryer basket when you are ready to bake them. Cook for 8 minutes at 400 F.

Step 6. Bacon pieces and the remaining 1/4 cup of cheddar cheese are sprinkled on top of the potatoes. While doing this, take care not to contact the hot surfaces of the air fryer basket.

# Quesadillas Air fryer

**Prep : 2 minutes / Cook Time : 8 minutes / Total Time : 15 mins**
**Servings 2**

## Ingredients

- 2 flour tortillas
- 43g cheese, more if desired
- Guacamole
- Greek yogurt
- 4 tablespoons refried beans, more if desired
- Optional toppings
- Sour cream
- Salsa

## Directions

Step 1. On a level surface, place the tortilla. Refried beans are spread throughout one-half of the tortilla. Cheese should be added to the beans.

Step 2. Half-fold the tortilla. With the remaining tortilla, repeat the procedure.Give each tortilla room to breathe as you place them in the air fryer basket.

Step 3. At 350 degrees Fahrenheit, air fried them for eight minutes, turning them over halfway through. The tortillas must be crisp and golden, and the cheese must be melted.

Step 4. Serve the quesadilla right away plain or topped with salsa, guacamole, sour cream, and Greek yogurt. Enjoy!

# breakfast Chocolate Chip Oatmeal Cookies

**Prep : 10 minutes / Cook Time : 7 minutes / Total Time : 17 mins**
**Servings 48 coockies**

## Ingredients

- 300g cup brown sugar
- 128g butter, melted
- 2 teaspoons vanilla extract
- 1 teaspoon baking soda
- 3/4 teaspoon salt
- 170g semisweet chocolate chips
- 100g granulated sugar
- 2 large eggs
- 420g all-purpose flour
- 1 teaspoon cinnamon
- 255 old fashioned rolled oats

## Directions

Step 1. In a mixing dish, combine the melted butter and both sugars. Blend well by beating.

Step 2. Add the vanilla essence and the eggs. a good beat Salt, cinnamon, baking soda, and flour should be sifted over the batter and thoroughly mixed. Add the chocolate chips and rolled oats by stirring.

Step 3. Use a sheet of tin foil or parchment paper to line the air fryer's basket.Put cookie dough balls the size of walnuts in the air fryer basket. Place them 1 to 2 inches apart, then softly press them to flatten them.

Step 4. Set the temperature to 300°F and close the air fryer basket. For 7 minutes, cook.Set on a wire rack to cool.

# Frozen Waffles air fryer

**Prep : 1 minute / Cook Time : 5 minutes / Total Time : 6 mins**
**Servings 2**

## Ingredients
• 4 frozen waffles

## Directions
Step 1. In the air fryer basket, put frozen waffles. Avoid piling on top of one another.

Step 2. Cook for three minutes at 350°F. After 2-3 minutes, flip the waffles over and continue cooking.

Step 3. Remove from basket with care, then serve.

# Air fryer Oatmeal

**Prep : 2 minutes / Cook Time : 15 minutes / Total Time : 17 mins**
**Servings 2**

## Ingredients
• 85g old fashioned oats
• 255g milk
• Additional Ingredients optional
• ¼ teaspoon ground cinnamon

• 340g water
• 1 pinch salt
• 2 to 3 tablespoons brown sugar

## Directions
Step 1. Use nonstick spray to grease a 6-inch round cake pan.

Step 2. Salt, milk, water, and oats should all be added to the pan and stirred.

Step 3. For 15 minutes, preheat the air fryer to 300°F. When the pan is hot, put it in the air fryer basket and cook it there until the time is up. (There is no need to stir during cooking.)

Step 4. Once cooked, carefully remove the pan from the air fryer (use oven mitts or kitchen towels; the pan will be HOT) and set it on a wire rack. Add cinnamon and brown sugar, stirring well after each addition. Allow the mixture to sit for about 5 minutes to thicken.

Step 5. Serve with fresh berries and chopped walnuts on top.

## Crusted Chicken Tenders air fryer

**Prep : 15 minutes / Cook Time : 15 minutes / Total Time : 30 mins**
**Servings 4**

### Ingredients

- 3 tablespoons all-purpose flour
- ¼ teaspoon freshly ground black pepper
- 3 ½ ounces salted pretzels, crushed
- 680g chicken tenderloins
- ¼ teaspoon ground turmeric
- ¼ teaspoon mustard powder
- 1 large egg, beaten
- olive oil cooking spray

### Directions

Step 1. Set the Ninja Foodi air fryer at 400 degrees Fahrenheit (200 degrees C).

Step 2. Combine the flour, mustard powder, turmeric, black pepper, and it in a large zip-top plastic bag. Shake the bag after sealing it after completely combining the dry Ingredients.

Step 3. On one plate, scatter the crushed pretzels. On a another plate, place the parchment paper. Add the chicken tenders to the bag of seasoned flour after patting them dry with paper towels. After shaking the tenders to coat them lightly, reseal the bag.

Step 4.With your clean non-dominant hand, throw pretzels onto the top of each tender after dipping it into the egg and brushing off the excess. Put a few pretzels that have been crushed inside each tender.Each pretzel-coated tender should be placed on the parchment-lined dish. On both sides, apply cooking spray with olive oil.

Step 5. In the air fryer that has been preheated, arrange the chicken tenders in a single layer. For 6 minutes, air fry. After 5 to 6 minutes of air frying, the chicken shouldn't be pink at the bone and the fluids should run clear. Using tongs, gently rotate the tenders.

## Lemon-Garlic Butter Lobster Tails

**Prep : 10 minutes / Cook Time : 10 minutes / Total Time : 20 mins**
**Servings 2**

### Ingredients

- 2 (113g) lobster tails
- 1 clove garlic, grated
- 1 teaspoon chopped fresh parsley
- 4 tablespoons butter
- salt and ground black pepper to taste
- 2 wedges lemon
- 1 teaspoon lemon zest

### Directions

Step 1. Set the air fryer to 380°F (195 degrees C). Create b utterfly lobster tails by cutting through the centers of the flesh and hard top shells longitudinally with kitchen shears. Cut up to but not past the bases of the shells. Distribute the tail parts. Place the lobster meat, facing up, in the air fryer basket with the tails.

Step 2. In a small saucepan over medium heat, melt the butter. Heat the lemon zest and garlic for 30 seconds, or until the garlic becomes aromatic. 2 tablespoons of the butter mixture should be brushed onto the lobster tails.

Step 3. Discard any remaining brushed butter to minimize cross-contamination with raw lobster. Season the lobster generously with salt and pepper.

Step 4. Cook for 7 minutes in a prepared Ninja Foodi air fryer, or until the lobster meat is opaque.

Step 5. Pour the remaining saucepan of butter over the lobster meat. Serve with lemon wedges and garnish with parsley.

# Lemon-Garlic Butter Lobster Tails

**Prep : 10 minutes / Cook Time : 10 minutes / Total Time : 20 mins**
**Servings 2**

## Ingredients

- 2 (113g) lobster tails
- 1 clove garlic, grated
- 1 teaspoon chopped fresh parsley
- 4 tablespoons butter
- salt and ground black pepper to taste
- 2 wedges lemon
- 1 teaspoon lemon zest

## Directions

Step 1. Set the air fryer to 380°F (195 degrees C). Create b utterfly lobster tails by cutting through the centers of the flesh and hard top shells longitudinally with kitchen shears. Cut up to but not past the bases of the shells. Distribute the tail parts. Place the lobster meat, facing up, in the air fryer basket with the tails. Melt the butter in a small saucepan set over medium heat.

Step 2. Heat the lemon zest and garlic for 30 seconds, or until the garlic gets fragrant. 2 tablespoons of the butter mixture should be brushed onto the lobster tails. Discard any remaining brushed butter to minimize cross-contamination with raw lobster. Season the lobster generously with salt and pepper.

Step 3. Cook for 7 minutes in a prepared Ninja Foodi air fryer, or until the lobster meat is opaque. Pour the remaining saucepan of butter over the lobster meat. Serve with lemon wedges and garnish with parsley.

# Air fryer Chicken Tenderloins

**Prep : 15 minutes / Cook Time : 12 minutes / Total Time : 27 mins**
**Servings 4**

## Ingredients

- 1 large egg
- 2 tablespoons vegetable oil
- 64g dry bread crumbs
- 8 chicken tenderloins

## Directions

Step 1. Preheat an air fryer to 350°F (175 degrees C).

Step 2. In a small dish, whisk the egg, then in a separate bowl, combine the bread crumbs and oil until the mixture is loose and crumbly. Dip each chicken tenderloin into the egg, shaking off any excess.

Step 3. Dip the chicken into the crumb mixture, covering it evenly and completely.

Step 4. Place the chicken tenderloins in the ninja foodi air fryer basket.

Step 5. Cook until the center of the chicken tenderloin is no longer pink, approximately 12 minutes. Serve and enjoy.

# Air fryer Crumbed Fish

**Prep : 10 minutes / Cook Time : 15 minutes / Total Time : 25 mins**
**Servings 4**

## Ingredients

- 128g dry bread crumbs
- 1 egg, beaten
- 85g vegetable oil
- 1 lemon, sliced
- 4 flounder fillets

## Directions

Step 1. Preheat an air fryer to 350°F (180 degrees C). In a small dish, combine the bread crumbs and oil. Stir until the mixture is loose and crumbly.

Step 2. Shake off any excess egg from the fish fillets. Coat the fillets evenly and completely in the bread crumb mixture.

Step 3. Place the coated fillets gently in the ninja Foodi air fryer basket, cook in the prepared air fryer for 12 minutes. Garnish with lemon slices and serve.

# Blackened Chicken Breast

**Prep : 10 minutes / Cook Time : 20 minutes / Total Time : 30 mins**
**Servings 2**

## Ingredients

- 2 tsp paprika
- 1 tsp cumin
- ½ tsp onion powder
- ¼ tsp salt
- 1 tsp ground thyme
- ½ tsp cayenne pepper
- ½ tsp black pepper
- 2 tsp vegetable oil
- 2 (340g) skinless, boneless chicken breast halves

## Directions

Step 1. In a mixing bowl, combine the paprika, thyme, cumin, cayenne pepper, onion powder, black pepper, and salt. Place spice mixture on a flat dish.

Step 2. Coat each chicken breast with oil. Roll each piece of chicken in the blackening spice mixture, pressing down to ensure the spice adheres to all sides. Allow it rest for 5 minutes while you warm the air fryer.

Step 3. Preheat an air fryer to 360°F (175°C) for 5 minutes.

Step 4. Cook the chicken for 10 minutes in the air fryer basket. Cook for an additional 10 minutes on the other side. Transfer the chicken to a platter and set aside for 5 minutes before serving.

# Blackened Chicken Breast

**Prep : 15 minutes / Cook Time : 15 minutes / Total Time : 30 mins**
**Servings 3**

## Ingredients

- 1 (411g) can salmon, drained and flaked
- 96g panko bread crumbs
- 113g mayonnaise
- 1 teaspoon dried dill weed
- salt and freshly ground black pepper to taste

- 1 large egg, beaten
- 64g diced onion
- ½ lemon, juiced
- 1 teaspoon seafood seasoning
- avocado oil nonstick cooking spray

## Directions

Step 1. In a bowl, mix the salmon, egg, panko, onions, mayonnaise, dill, lemon juice, seafood spice, and salt and pepper. After thoroughly combining, form into 6 equal patties.

Step 2. Set the air fryer to 400 degrees Fahrenheit (200 degrees C). Spray avocado oil on the parchment paper before lining the air fryer basket.

Step 3. Spray avocado oil over the basket and add the salmon croquettes.

Step 4. For 8 to 10 minutes, air fried croquettes until golden brown. Croquettes should be turned over, sprayed with avocado oil, and air-fried for a further 4 to 7 minutes. Whenever required, cook in batches.

# Air fryer Cajun Salmon

**Prep : 10 minutes / Cook Time : 10 minutes / Total Time : 20 mins**
**Servings 2**

## Ingredients

- 2 (170g) skin-on salmon fillets
- 1 tablespoon Cajun seasoning

- cooking spray
- 1 teaspoon brown sugar

## Directions

Step 1. The air fryer should be preheated to 390 degrees F. (200 degrees C). Dry off salmon fillets with a paper towel after rinsing. Mist fillets with cooking spray then add the Cajun spice and brown sugar in a small dish.

Step 2. Fillet flesh sides are pressed into the spice mixture after being sprinkled onto a dish.

Step 3. Salmon fillets should be placed skin-side down in the air fryer's basket after being sprayed with cooking spray. Spray cooking spray on the fish once more sparingly.

Step 4. Cook for 8 minutes. Before serving, remove from the air fryer and let it two minutes to rest.

# Turkey breast Air fryer

**Prep : 10 minutes / Cook Time : 40 minutes / Total Time : 1 hrs**
**Servings 6**

## Ingredients

- 1 tablespoon chopped fresh rosemary
- 1 teaspoon minced fresh garlic
- ¼ teaspoon ground black pepper, or to taste
- 1.2kg skin-on, bone-in split turkey breast
- 1 teaspoon chopped fresh chives
- ½ teaspoon salt or to taste
- 2 tablespoons cold unsalted butter

## Directions

Step 1. On a chopping board, arrange the rosemary, chives, garlic, salt, and pepper. Herbs and seasonings are topped with thinly sliced butter, which is then mashed until completely combined.

Step 2. Dry off the turkey breast by patting it, then massage it all over, including under the skin, with herbed butter. Turkey should be placed skin-side down in the air fryer basket and cooked for 20 minutes.

Step 3. Carefully flip the turkey over to the skin-side-up position and continue to fry for an additional 18 minutes, or until an instant-read thermometer placed close to the bone registers 165 degrees F (74 degrees C).

Step 4. Tent with aluminum foil and transfer to a dish; let sit for 10 minutes. Slice and warmly serve.

# Air Fryer Breaded Pork Chops

**Prep : 10 minutes / Cook Time : 10 minutes / Total Time : 20 mins**
**Servings 4**

## Ingredients

- 4 (140g) boneless, center-cut pork chops, 1-inch thick
- 128g cheese and garlic croutons
- cooking spray
- 1 teaspoon Cajun seasoning
- 2 large eggs

## Directions

Step 1. Set an air fryer at 400 degrees Fahrenheit (200 degrees C). On a platter, spread some Cajun spice over the pork chops.

Step 2. Place the croutons on a shallow plate after finely pulverizing them in a small food processor. Put eggs in a small plate and lightly beat them. Pork chops should be breaded one at a time by dipping them into beaten egg, letting excess drop off, pressing them into crouton breading to cover both sides, and then placing them, unstacked, on a platter.

Step 3. Keep going with the remaining chops. Chops are sprayed with frying spray. Chops are arranged in a single layer in theninja foodi air fryer basket after being sprayed with cooking spray.

Step 4. Cook for 5 minutes in the prepared air fryer. Flip the chops over, and if necessary, remist with frying spray any dry spots. 5 more minutes of cooking. The chops' internal temperature should register 145 degrees Fahrenheit on an instant-read thermometer (63 degrees C).

# Mustard-Crusted Pork Tenderloin

Prep : 10 minutes / Cook Time : 30 minutes / Total Time : 40 mins
Servings 4

## Ingredients

- 85g Dijon mustard
- 1 teaspoon dried parsley flakes
- ¼ teaspoon salt
- 569g pork tenderloin
- 1 (340g) package fresh green beans, trimmed
- salt and ground black pepper to taste
- cooking spray
- 2 tablespoons brown sugar
- ½ teaspoon dried thyme
- ¼ teaspoon ground black pepper
- ¾ pound small potatoes halved
- 1 tablespoon olive oil
- 2 large eggs

## Directions

Step 1. Set a 400°F air fryer temperature (200 degrees C). In a large bowl, combine the mustard, brown sugar, parsley, thyme, salt, and pepper. The tenderloin should be well coated on both sides after being rolled in the mustard mixture. In a another bowl, combine the potatoes, green beans, and olive oil. Stir in the appropriate amounts of salt and pepper after seasoning to taste. Place aside.

Step 2. Place the tenderloin in the basket of the prepared air fryer, and cook it for about 20 minutes, without moving it, until the middle is just beginning to become pink. In the middle, an instant-read thermometer should register at least 145 degrees Fahrenheit (63 degrees C). Place on a chopping board and let for 10 minutes to rest.

Step 3. Potatoes and green beans should be placed in the other air fryer basket of your Ninja Foodi Due air fryer. Cook for 10 minutes, shaking the air fryer basket halfway through. Along with potatoes and green beans, slice the tenderloin and serve.

# Mustard-Crusted Pork Tenderloin

Prep : 5 minutes / Cook Time : 10 minutes / Additional Time:4 hrs 35 mins
Total Time : 4 hrs 50 mins / Servings 4

## Ingredients

- 453g beef sirloin steak, cut into 1-inch cubes
- 85g Worcestershire sauce
- 1 teaspoon parsley flakes
- 1 teaspoon crushed chile flakes
- 226g button mushrooms, sliced
- 1 tablespoon olive oil
- 1 teaspoon paprika

## Directions

Step 1. In a bowl, combine the steak, mushrooms, Worcestershire sauce, extra virgin olive oil, parsley, paprika, and chili flakes.

Step 2. Overnight or for at least 4 hours, cover and chill. 30 minutes before cooking, remove from refrigerator.

Step 3. Set an air fryer at 400 degrees Fahrenheit (200 degrees C).

Step 4. From the steak combination, drain and toss the marinade. In the air fryer's basket, put the steak and the mushrooms.

Step 5. Five minutes of cooking in the preheated air fryer. Five more minutes of cooking after a toss. Place the steak and mushrooms on a serving platter and give them time to rest for five minutes.

# Coconut Shrimp

**Prep : 30 minutes / Cook Time : 15 minute / Total Time : 45 mins**
**Servings 6**

## Ingredients

- 68g all-purpose flour
- 2 large eggs
- 43g panko bread crumbs
- cooking spray
- 85g honey
- 1 serrano chile, thinly sliced

- 1 ½ teaspoons ground black pepper
- 85g unsweetened flaked coconut
- 340g uncooked medium shrimp, peeled and deveined
- ½ teaspoon kosher salt, divided
- 85l lime juice
- 2 teaspoons chopped fresh cilantro

## Directions

Step 1. In a small bowl, combine the flour and pepper. In a separate shallow bowl, lightly beat eggs. In a third shallow dish, combine the coconut and panko. Dredge shrimp in flour mixture, one at a time, and brush off extra. Toss the floured shrimp in the egg and let any extra fall off.

Step 2. Last but not least, dredge in coconut mixture and press to adhere. Organize the shrimp on a platter. Apply cooking spray liberally to shrimp.

Step 3. Set the air fryer to 400 degrees Fahrenheit (200 degrees C). Cook the shrimp for about 3 minutes after adding half of them to the air fryer. After 3 minutes, flip the shrimp over and continue to cook until golden. Add 1/4 teaspoon of salt to the dish. Repeat with the rest of the shrimp.

Step 4. In the meantime, combine lime juice, honey, and serrano chile in a small dish.

Step 5. Add cilantro to the fried shrimp before serving with the honey-lime dip.

**Prep : 15 min / Cook Time : 15 min / Total Time : 30 mins**
**Servings 4**

## Ingredients

- 1kg octopus, thawed
- 1/4 cup kebab powder
- 2 tablespoons virgin oil

- 1/2 lime
- 2 teaspoons crushed garlic
- Lime wedges to serve

- 1 tablespooon parsley flakes
- 2 teaspoosn ground ginger

## Directions

Step 1. Along with your seafood boil, add butter and seasonings to the Air Fryer Basket.

Step 2. Set the temperature to 400 degrees F, air fryer setting for 8 to 10 minutes. The key is to shake the basket frequently during the cooking process. Enjoy! Serve immediately!

# Prawn and kingfish ceviche

**Prep : 10 minutes / Cook Time : 2 minutes / Total Time : 12 mins**
**Servings 6**

## Ingredients
- 200g peeled green prawns, deveined
- 1 thinly sliced red onion
- 200g skinless sashimi-grade kingfish fillet pin-boned, cut into 1cm pieces
- 1 crushed garlic clove
- 1 finely chopped green chilli
- 2 tbsp finely chopped coriander
- 250ml lime juice
- 2 tbsp extra virgin olive oil
- Rye bread croutons optional

## Directions
Step 1. Soak the onion in a dish of cold water for 10 minutes. Drain and set aside.

Step 2. Meanwhile, bring a small saucepan of water to a simmer over medium-low heat. Blanch the prawns for 1 minute or until almost cooked through. Drain, refresh, then chop into 1cm pieces.

Step 3. Place the kingfish in a ceramic or glass bowl with the chopped prawn, garlic, chilli and coriander. Season the mixture, then add 5 ice cubes and enough lime juice to just barely cover it.

Step 4. Add one-third of the onion and mix to incorporate — the lime juice should develop a yellowish tint after a few seconds. Taste the ceviche and adjust the seasonings.

Step 5. After removing the ice cubes, add the oil and stir. Garnish with the remaining onion and serve with croutons.

**Prep : 40 min / Cook Time : 40 min / Total Time : 1 hour and 20 mins**
**Servings 4**

## Ingredients
- 60grams unsalted butter
- 1 finely leek (chopped )
- 1 finely garlic clove (chopped )
- 400g green prawns (peeled)
- 125ml dry white wine
- 300ml thickened cream
- 2 tbsp lemon juice
- 1 tbsp plain flour
- 1 tsp Dijon mustard
- 3 sheets frozen puff pastry, thawed
- 185ml fish stock
- 1 tbsp fresh dill (chopped)
- 1 tbsp flat-leaf parsley (chopped)
- 1 egg yolk mixed with 1 tbsp water (To brush)

## Directions
Step 1. Melt the butter in a saucepan over low heat. Add the leek and garlic and simmer, stirring, for 2-3 minutes until softened.

Step 2. Add the prawns to the pan after seasoning. Stir for 2 minutes or until just done, then remove the prawns with a slotted spoon and put aside.

Step 3 . Add flour to the pan and cook, stirring, for 1 minute. Add stock and wine and whisk to remove any lumps. Increase heat to medium then cook for 10 minutes or until liquid has reduced.

Step 4. After adding the cream, simmer the mixture for a further 10 minutes, or until it thickens and reduces by half. Remove from the heat and allow it cool slightly. Add lemon juice, herbs and mustard, then return the prawns to the mixture. Season, then fully cool.

Step 5. Preheat oven to 200°C. Egg wash should be applied to pastry lids. Pies should be baked for 12 to 15 minutes, or until the pastry is cooked through and golden.

# Air fry Prawn party pies

**Prep : 40 min / Cook Time : 40 min / Total Time : 1 hour and 20 mins**
**Servings 4**

## Ingredients

- 60grams unsalted butter
- 1 finely garlic clove (chopped )
- 125ml dry white wine
- 2 tbsp lemon juice
- 1 tsp Dijon mustard
- 185ml fish stock
- 1 tbsp flat-leaf parsley (chopped)

- 1 finely leek (chopped )
- 400g green prawns (peeled)
- 300ml thickened cream
- 1 tbsp plain flour
- 3 sheets frozen puff pastry, thawed
- 1 tbsp fresh dill (chopped)
- 1 egg yolk mixed with 1 tbsp water (To brush)

## Directions

Step 1. Melt the butter in a saucepan over low heat. Add the leek and garlic and simmer, stirring, for 2-3 minutes until softened.

Step 2. Add the prawns to the pan after seasoning. Stir for 2 minutes or until just done, then remove the prawns with a slotted spoon and put aside.

Step 3 . Add flour to the pan and cook, stirring, for 1 minute. Add stock and wine and whisk to remove any lumps. Increase heat to medium then cook for 10 minutes or until liquid has reduced.

Step 4. After adding the cream, simmer the mixture for a further 10 minutes, or until it thickens and reduces by half. Remove from the heat and allow it cool slightly. Add lemon juice, herbs and mustard, then return the prawns to the mixture. Season, then fully cool.

Step 5. Preheat air fryer to 360°C. Egg wash should be applied to pastry lids. Pies should be cooked for 12 to 15 minutes, or until the pastry is cooked through and golden.

# Air fryer boiled seafood

**Prep : 10 min / Cook Time : 10 min / Total Time : 20 mins**
**Servings 1**

## Ingredients

- 1 Fresh Corn of Cob, Cut in Half
- 2 Lobster tails, cut in half
- Salt & Black Pepper

- 227g fresh shrimp
- 2 tablespoons butter
- Old Bay Seasoning or Cajun

## Directions

Step 1. Along with your seafood boil, add butter and seasonings to the Air Fryer Basket.

Step 2. Set the temperature to 400 degrees F, air fryer setting for 8 to 10 minutes. The key is to shake the basket frequently during the cooking process. Enjoy! Serve immediately!

# Kebab Octopus Air fryer

**Prep : 15 min / Cook Time : 15 min / Total Time : 30 mins**

**Servings 4**

## Ingredients

- 1kg octopus, thawed
- 1 tablespooon parsley flakes
- 2 teaspoons crushed garlic
- 2 tablespoons virgin oil
- 1/2 lime
- 1/4 cup kebab powder
- 2 teaspoosn ground ginger
- Lime wedges to serve

## Directions

Step 1. Along with your seafood boil, add butter and seasonings to the Air Fryer Basket.

Step 2. Set the temperature to 400 degrees F, air fryer setting for 8 to 10 minutes. The key is to shake the basket frequently during the cooking process. Enjoy! Serve immediately!

# Air Fryer Mussels Dynamite

**Prep : 5 min / Cook Time : 8 min / Total Time : 13 mins**

**Servings 2**

## Ingredients

- 12 green mussels defrosted

**Sauce Ingredients**
- 85g Kewpie mayonnaise
- ¼ tsp salt
- ½ tsp sugar

- 1 – 1½ tbsp tobiko

- 42g Parmesan cheese
- 1 tsp Sriracha
- 1 tsp lime juice

## Directions

Step 1. Mix all of the sauce's components together in a bowl. Put the mussels in the air fryer basket after lining it with aluminum foil (optional).

Step 2. Top each mussel with the sauce mixture.

Step 3. for eight minutes, air fry at 350 °F (or until sauce is slightly brown). Keep in mind that every air fryer operates differently, so consult your instructions for the right temperature and duration.

Step 4. Remove mussels and top with tobiko. Enjoy immediately!

# Spicy Garlic Prawns

Prep : 5 min / Cook Time : 7 min / Total Time : 12 mins
Servings 3

## Ingredients

- 15 Fresh prawns
- 1 tsp Chili powder
- 1 tbsp Sweet chilli sauce
- 1/2 tsp Salt
- 1 1/2 tbsp Olive oil
- 1 tsp Black pepper
- 1 clove Garlic, minced

## Directions

Step 1. Prawns should be washed and rinsed. Preheat the air fryer at 360°F. The prawns should be put in a mixing dish.

Step 2. Add oil, chili sauce, garlic, black pepper, and chili powder to the bowl. Until the prawns are well coated, stir and combine the Ingredients. To taste, add salt.

Step 3. Prawns should be put in the air fryer and let cook for 5 to 7 minutes.

Step 4. After 5 minutes check the prawns and give them a toss. To sop up the mouthwatering sauce, serve the prawns in a spicy garlic sauce over rice.

# COD Parmesan air fry

Prep : 10 minutes / Cook Time : 15 minutes / Total Time : 25 mins
Servings 4 COD

## Ingredients

- 450g cod filets
- 68g flour
- 1/2 teaspoon salt
- 43g cup grated parmesan
- 1/2 teaspoon garlic powder
- salt and pepper
- 2 large eggs
- 136g Panko
- 2 teaspoons old bay seasoning
- olive oil to drizzle if needed

## Directions

Step 1. Cod filets should be salted and peppered. Make a station for breading fish. Add the flour to a bowl. The eggs and salt should be combined in the second bowl. Add the Panko, parmesan cheese, old bay seasoning, and garlic powder to the final bowl.

Step 2. Cod should first be floured. After that, add the egg mixture. Finally, in the Panko.

Step 3. Drizzle the bottom of your ninja foodi basket with olive oil. Put the fish in the air fryer's basket. Cook at 400 degrees for 10 minutes. Flip the fish gently. Cook the meat for an additional 3–5 minutes, or until it reaches a temperature of 145 degrees, inside.

# Salmon garlic brown sugar

Prep : 5 minutes / Cook Time : 10 minutes / Total Time : 15 mins

**Servings 4**

## Ingredients
- 453g salmon
- 1 tsp chili powder
- 1 tsp Italian seasoning
- salt and pepper
- 2 tsp brown sugar
- 1/2 tsp paprika
- 1 tsp garlic powder

## Directions
Step 1. The salmon should be seasoned. Add the brown sugar in a small bowl, chili powder, paprika, Italian seasoning and garlic powder. On the salmon, rub.

Step 2. In the basket of your ninja foodi air fryer place the salmon skin side down. Turn the ninja foodi air fryer to 400 degrees and cook the salmon for 10 minutes.

# Walleye Air Fry
**Prep : 6 minutes / Cook Time : 10 minutes / Total Time : 16 mins**
**Servings 2**

## Ingredients
- 4 walleye fillets
- 85g bag of pork rinds I used Old Dutch
- ¼ tsp cayenne pepper
- 1 large egg
- 1 tsp garlic powder
- 1 lemon cut into 8 wedges

## Directions
Step 1. Crush the pork rinds into crumbs. I dump them into a gallon bag and roll over them with a rolling pin until nice and crumbly.

Step 2. The gallon bag of pork rind crumbs should now include 14 teaspoon of cayenne and 1 teaspoon of garlic powder. Shake to mix. Pour the pork rind crumbs onto a dish.

Step 3. Crack one egg into a bowl and whisk until the white and yolk are mixed.Make sure both sides of a walleye fillet are coated by dipping it into the whisked eggs. Allow any extra egg to drip off.

Step 4. Put the walleye fillet through a thorough coating of pork rind crumbs on both sides.Spray a dab of cooking spray on the rack in your air fryer to ensure the fillets don't cling.

Step 5. Crush the pork rinds into crumbs then put the walleye fillets on the air fryer rack. Use the remaining fillets as a model.

Step 6. Air Fry at 400 degrees Fahrenheit for roughly 10 minutes. When halfway through flip walleye, if needed. Serve with lemon wedges.

# White fish crusted garlic Parmesan
**Prep : 10 minutes / Cook Time : 15 minutes / Total Time : 25 mins**
**Servings 2**

## Ingredients
- 2 White fish (about 170g for each filet)
- 15 ml olive oil , or oil spray

- 50 g grated parmesan cheese
- black pepper , to taste
- 2.5 ml onion powder
- Chopped parsley and lemon wedges for serving
- kosher salt , to taste
- 2.5 ml garlic powder
- 2.5 ml smoked paprika (To taste)

## Directions

Step 1. For five minutes, preheat the Ninja Foodi Air Fryer to 380°F/193°C. Put the parmesan in a small bowl & set aside.

Step 2. Drizzle olive oil generously over fish or sprinkle with oil spray. Season with garlic powder, salt, onion powder, pepper & paprika. Press fish into the cheese mixture and coat all sides of the fish filets.

Step 3. Use perforated parchment paper to line the air fryer basket or tray. Lightly spray parchment paper with oil spray.

Step 4. Lay coated fish on the parchment. Lightly coat the top of the fish filets with oil spray.

Step 5. Air Fry at 380°F/193°C for about 8-12 minutes, or until you can flaked it with a fork. Depending on the thickness of the fish and the design of your air fryer, cooking times will change.

Step 6. Served with lemon wedges and chopped parsley.

# air fried Haddock

**Prep : 10 minutes / Cook Time : 10 minutes / Total Time : 20 mins**
**Servings 4**

## Ingredients

- 4 pieces haddock fish (140g each)
- 1 teaspoon salt
- 255g panko bread crumbs
- 6 tablespoons mayonnaise
- 68g all purpose flour
- 1/2 teaspoon black pepper
- 2 eggs
- tartar sauce and lemon wedges optional

## Directions

Step 1. Start by mixing a small mixing bowl the panko breadcrumbs, salt, and pepper. In a second bowl, pour the flour. In the third bowl, mayonnaise and egg should be mix together.

Step 2. Dip the haddock fish into the flour, then into the egg or mayo mixture, and finally into the panko mixture. After you dip them in the mixture, place them in a greased ninja foodi air fryer basket or a greased air fryer tray.

Step 3. When you finish breading your fish, drizzle generously with olive oil spray. For 8 to 12 minutes, place the tray or basket into the air fryer set to 350 degrees Fahrenheit.

Step 4. Remove your fish after it flakes easily. Serve with tartar sauce and/or lemon wedges. Enjoy! Plate and serve!

# Tuna Patties

**Prep : 10 minutes / Cook Time : 15 minutes / Total Time : 25 mins**
**Servings 10 patties**

## Ingredients

- 425 g canned albacore tuna or fresh tune (diced)
- 1 medium lemon (zest)
- 55 g bread crumbs
- 1 stalk celery , finely chopped
- 2.5 ml garlic powder
- 1.25 ml Kosher salt or to taste
- Ranch or tarter sauce (optional)

- 2-3 large eggs
- 15 ml lemon juice
- 45 ml grated parmesan cheese
- 45 ml minced onion
- 2.5 ml dried herbs (oregano, dill, basil)
- black pepper fresh cracked

## Directions

Step 1. Inside a medium bowl, whisk the eggs, lemon zest, celery, onion, garlic powder,  lemon juice, bread crumbs, parmesan cheese, dried herbs, salt and pepper. Mix to make absolutely sure it's all combined. Gently press in the tuna until just mixed.

Step 2. Try to keep all patties equal size and thickness for uniform cooking. Scoop out 1/4 cup of the mixture, form patties that are about 3 inches wide and 1/2 inch thick, and then place them inside the basket. Makes about 10 patties.

Step 3. If patties are too loose to handle, chill them for at about 1 hour or till firm. It will make them simpler to handle all through cooking. Spritz or brush the top of the patties with oil.

Step 4. Lay perforated air fryer baking sheet or perforated silicone mat within base of air fryer.

Step 5. Mist the paper or mat sparingly.

Step 6.  Air Fry at 360°F for 6 minutes. Turn the patties and spritz the tops once more with oil. Keep going to Air Fry for a further 3-5 minutes or till cooked to your liking. Start serving with your preferred sauce and lemon wedges.

# Miso Glazed chilean Sea Bass

**Prep :  5 minutes / Cook Time : 20 minutes / Total Time : 25 mins**

**Servings 2**

## Ingredients

- 2 (170g each) chilean sea bass fillets
- 84g white miso paste
- 4 tbsp maple syrup
- 1/2 tbsp  ginger paste
- fresh cracked pepper

- 1 tbsp unsalted butter
- 1 tbsp rice wine vinegar
- 2 tbsp  mirin
- olive oil for cooking
- sesame seeds and sliced green onions- Optional toppings

## Directions

Step 1. Set ninja foodi air fryer to 375° F. Each fish fillet should be coated in olive oil, then garnished with freshly cracked pepper.

Step 2. Sprinkle the air fryer pan with olive oil and put the fish skin side down. Cook for 13-15 minutes, until the top starts to turn golden brown and the core temperature has achieved 135° F.

Step 3. While each fish is cooking, melt the butter in a small saucepan on a medium heat. Whenever the butter has melted, add the miso paste, maple syrup, maple syrup, mirin,  rice wine vinegar and ginger paste.

Step 4. As soon as the mixture is thoroughly combined, turn off the heat and remove the pan from it.

Step 5. When the fish is ready, use a silicone pastry brush to glaze over the top and sides of the fish. Put it back in the ninja foodi air fryer for 1-2 more minutes at 375° F, till the glaze caramelizes. Finish with sesame seeds or thinly sliced green onions.

# Sweet and Spicy Salmon

**Prep : 6 minutes / Cook Time : 8 minutes / Total Time : 14 mins**
**Servings 4**

## Ingredients

- 4 salmon fillets
- 3/4 tsp chili powder
- 1/2 tsp garlic powder
- 1/2 tsp salt

- 3 tbsphoney
- 3/4 tsp paprika
- 1/2 tsp crushed red pepper flakes
- 1/4 tsp pepper

## Directions

Step 1. Pat dry salmon with paper towels. Spritz the ninja foodi air fryer basket with oil and put salmon in the basket.

Step 2. Put honey and the remaining Ingredients in a small bowl. Microwave for 10 seconds, Mix and paint on the salmon fillets. Air fry at 390 degrees for 8 minutes.

# Sweet and Spicy Salmon

**Prep : 10 minutes / Cook Time : 13 minutes / Total Time : 23 mins**
**Servings 4**

## Ingredients

- 1 egg
- 453g cod fillets (about 4 fillets)
- 2 tbsp all purpose flour
- 1 tsp garlic powder
- 1/2 tspsalt

- 2 tbsp water
- 128g panko breadcrumbs
- 1 tsp paprika
- 1/2 tsp fresh thyme
- extra-virgin olive oil drizzle

## Directions

Step 1. Mix water and egg in a bowl and mix together. Then set aside.

Step 2. Chop the cod lengthwise and afterwards cut into nugget-likelike slices. Set aside. In medium bowl add panko, four, paprika, garlic powder then add salt. Add thyme and whisk herbs together.

Step 3. Dip the cod into egg wash. In a separate bowls with egg, bread crumbs and fish. Then dip into panko mixture, in a separate bowl with egg, bread crumbs and fish.

Step 4. Place in a basket lined with parchment paper or a crisper tray lined with paper. Pure extra virgin olive oil should be used for spraying. spraying olive oil on the nuggets.

## Pork Belly Bites

**Prep : 20 minutes / Cook Time : 20 minutes / Total Time : 40 mins**
**Servings 2**

### Ingredients
- 226g pork belly (patted dry)
- 1 tsp brown sugar
- 1 tsp salt
- 3 tbspcanola oil
- 1 tsp garlic powder
- 1 tsp pepper

### Directions
Step 1. Set the temperature of the air fryer to 400°F. Pat dry the pork belly then cut it into 1-inch pieces. In the meantime, combine the oil, brown sugar, garlic powder, salt, and pepper in a big bowl.

Step 2. Add the pork belly bits to the oil mixture, trying to cover each piece. Lay the pork belly chunks in a single layer in the ninja foodi air fryer basket.

Step 3. Air fry the pork belly cubes for 15-20 minutes, shaking and flipping them a few times throughout the cooking time. Remove from the ninja foodi air fryer and serve warm.

## Breaded pork chops

**Prep : 10 minutes / Cook Time : 8 minutes / Total Time : 18 mins**
**Servings 4**

### Ingredients
- 453g boneless pork chops (1/2-inch thick)
- 1/4 tsp black pepper
- 1 tsp garlic powder (divided)
- 2 large eggs
- 43g seasoned Italian breadcrumbs
- fresh chopped parsley (optional)
- 1/2 tsp kosher salt
- 68g all-purpose flour
- 1 tsp onion powder (divided)
- splash of water
- 43g grated parmesan cheese (plus more for garnish)

### Directions
Step 1. Season on the both sides of pork chops with the salt and pepper, then set aside.

Step 2. Mix the flour, 1/2 tsp of garlic powder, and 1 tsp of onion powder in a large bowl. In another bowl, carefully whisk together the eggs, splash of water, 1/2 tsp of the garlic powder, and 1 tsp of the onion powder. In the 3rd bowl, mix together the breadcrumbs and parmesan cheese.

Step 3. One by one, dip the pork chops into the flour mixture and coat completely. Shake off any extra flour, then dip into the egg mixture and coat completely.

Step 4. Shake off any excess breadcrumbs before placing the pork chop into the breadcrumb mixture and evenly coating. Let any excess egg drip off. The remaining pork chops should be repeated. If your air fryer requires preheating, set ninja foodi air fryer to 400°F for 5 minutes.

Step 5. Sprinkle the air fryer basket with cooking spray, add two pork chops in the basket or as many as you can fit without them touching. Drizzle cooking spray on top of the porkchops.

Step 6. Air fry for 4 minutes, turn them over, sprinkle the top with more frying spray and air fry an additional 4 minutes or until an internal temperature hits 145°F.If desired, garnish with additional grated parmesan cheese and parsley.

# Roast Boneless Pork

Prep : 10 minutes / Cook Time : 1 HOUR 10 minutes / Total Time : 1 HOUR 20 mins
Servings 4-6

## Ingredients

- 1.5kg Boneless Roast Pork Shoulder
- 1 tbsp Olive Oil
- 1-2 tbsp Coarse Salt

## Directions

Step 1. Take the roast out of the packing and any netting, then pat it dry using some paper towels. Score the rind with a small, sharp knife at 1-cm intervals, being careful not to cut into the meat. Request that your butcher score your rind instead.

Step 2. Leave the meat in the refrigerator overnight(but 1 hour will help dry the rind & assist in the crackling process).

Step 3. Olive oil should be applied evenly to the pork before roasting. The rind should then have a generous amount of salt added to it. Be sure to rub the salt into the scores.

Step 4. Place the roast in the ninja foodi air fryer basket with the rind facing up. Cook at 200°C (400°F) for 20 minutes, then at 180°C (350°F) for the final five minutes to ensure complete cooking (around 25 minutes for every 500g/lb).

Step 5. Move the roast to a carving board or plate & allow to rest for 10 minutes. Carve, then serve.

# Air fryer pork meatballs

Prep : 10 minutes / Cook Time : 15 minutes / Total Time : 25 mins
Servings 4

## Ingredients

- 453g ground pork
- 1 tsp salt
- 1/2 tsp black pepper
- 1 tsp smoked paprika
- 1/2 yellow onion
- 1/2 tsp mustard powder
- 1 tsp garlic powder

## Directions

Step 1. Begin by grating the onion into a mixing bowl, and then add the other Ingredients and ground pork

Use your hands to thoroughly combine the meat, onion, and seasonings.

Step 2. Place the 1-inch balls of pork mixture into the air fryer basket. Meatballs can be touching, but not jammed in together. If needed, apply the remaining few lightly on top of the bottom layer. Cook on 375 degrees F. for 15 minutes, turning halfway through.

Step 3. Take from the ninja foodi air fryer and serve with noodles, or on its own with vegetable sides.

# Beef Steak Tips

**Prep : 5 minutes / Cook Time : 9 minutes / Total Time : 14 mins**
**Servings 3**

## Ingredients

- 680g steak beef chuck (cut to 3/4 inch cubes)
- 1 tsp oil
- 1/2 tsp ground black pepper
- 1/2 tsp dried onion powder
- 1/8 tsp cayenne pepper
- 1/4 tsp salt
- Steak Marinade
- 1/4 tsp salt
- 1/2 tsp dried garlic powder
- 1 tsp Montreal Steak Seasoning
- 452g Asparagus (ends trimmed)
- 1/2 tsp oil (optional)

## Directions

Step 1. Set the temperature of the air fryer at 400F for about 5 minutes. Meanwhile, cut the steak of any fat and cut it into cubes. Then, stir with the Ingredients in a bowl for the marinate, add the oil, salt, black pepper, Montreal seasoning, onion and garlic powder & the cayenne pepper. Massage the spices into the meat to coat evenly. To make cleanup simpler, do this inside a ziplock bag.

Step 2. If you have any nonstick spray on hand, use it to coat the bottom of the air fryer basket before distributing the prepared meat across it.

Step 3. Cook the beef steak tips for about 6 minutes and check for desired consistency.

Step 4. When the asparagus is evenly coated, toss it with 1/2 teaspoon oil and 1/4 teaspoon salt.

Step 5. Toss the steak bites around and move them to one side when they are cooked to your preference. Add the asparagus to the other basket of the ninja foodi duo air fryer and cook for a further 3 minutes.

Step 6. Take the steak tips and the asparagus to a serving dish and serve while hot.

# Beef Meatball Sub Skewers

**Prep : 30 minutes / Cook Time : 10 minutes / Total Time : 40 mins**
**Servings 6**

## Ingredients

- 453g lean ground beef
- 32g fine breadcrumbs
- ½ tsp garlic powder
- ½ tsp kosher salt
- 1 large egg
- 2 tsp italian seasoning
- ½ tsp onion powder

- 3 mozzarella cheese sticks or 3oz of mozzarella cut into cubes
- 1 tube crescent roll dough 225g tube of 8 rolls
- 34g shredded parmesan cheese optional
- Optional Toppings
- 170g pizza sauce optional

**Garlic Herb Butter Ingredients**
- 57g butter melted
- ½ tsp garlic powder
- 1 tsp parsley flakes

## Directions

Step 1. Start by mixing the ground beef, breadcrumbs, Italian seasoning, onion powder, garlic powder and salt in a medium scale bowl. Mix until well blended.

Step 2. Sliced the cheese sticks so that you have 18 small cubes of cheese. Scoop about 1 ½ tablespoon of the beef mixture and shape into a ball, then compress slightly. Press a cheese cube into the center then wrap the beef all around cheese. You should have a meatball the size of a golf ball at the end. Continue with the remaining meat and cheese until there are 18 meatballs.

Step 3. Open the crescent roll dough and unroll onto a piece of parchment or wax paper. Pinch the seams before slicing the fabric into 1 14 inch wide strips.

Step 4. To start making the skewers, thread one end of a dough strip onto the tip of a skewer, after which add a meatball. Tie the dough over the meatball and onto the skewer. Place a second meatball on top and rewrap the dough around it. Add the third meatball, then wrap the dough's end around it to secure it to the skewer. This should look like 3 meatballs with the dough trying to wrap around in an S-like pattern.

Step 5. Press the meatballs down the skewer so you have roughly 1 inch of skewer at the top. The meatballs should then be slightly spaced apart to allow for dough expansion. Continually do this until you have 6 skewers.

Step 6. After five minutes of preheating the air fryer to 350°F, insert the skewers into the basket, leaving space for air to circulate and the dough to rise. At a time, I put three skewers in the basket of my 5.8-quart air fryer.

Step 7. Set the ninja foodi air fryer to 350°F and cook for 7-10 minutes until the meatballs are golden brown and the dough is puffed and golden. Continue with the remaining skewers.

Step 8. Make the garlic butter as the skewers cook. Remove the skewers from the basket once they are done cooking, brush with garlic butter, top with parmesan cheese, and serve.

# Cheeseburger Pockets

**Prep : 2 minutes / Cook Time : 10 minutes / Total Time : 12 mins**
**Servings 4**

## Ingredients
- 1 Can Biscuits (8 Count)
- Cheddar Cheese Shredded Sharp
- 453g Ground Beef Cooked

## Directions

Step 1. Remove the biscuits from the can and roll or flatten the dough with your hands to make it thin.

Step 2. Four of the flattened biscuits should be topped with some ground beef and cheddar cheese evenly distributed. Use another biscuit without the toppings and set it on top of the beef and cheese topped biscuit. Draw the dough to fully fit and form a pocket.

Step 3. By pressing it down around the edge, a fork can be used to seal the sides. Put each pocket in a greased ninja foodi air fryer basket, as many as will fit.

Step 4. Once placed in the air fryer, coat with olive oil cooking spray if wanted and then air fry at 360* for 5 minutes. Turn the pockets over carefully after the timer goes off.

Step 5. Air Fry a further 4-5 minutes at 360*F. Given that every air fryer heats differently, check on these after three to four minutes. When finished, they will become nicely browned.

# Beef Stuffed Peppers

**Prep : 15 minutes / Cook Time : 15 minutes / Total Time : 30 mins**

**Servings 4**

## Ingredients

- 6 Green Bell Peppers
- 1 Tbsp Olive Oil
- 32g Cup Fresh Parsley
- 340g Marinara Sauce More to Taste
- 1/2 Tsp Garlic Salt

- 453g Lean Ground Beef
- 32g Green Onion Diced
- 1/2 Tsp Ground Sage
- 21g Shredded Mozzarella Cheese
- 85g Cooked Rice

## Directions

Step 1. Ground beef should be heated in a medium-sized skillet and cooked to perfection. Returning the steak to the pan after draining.

Step 2. In a bowl, mix in the olive oil, green onion, parsley, sage, and salt. Add in the marinara and cooked rice, mix well.

Step 3. Remove the top off of each pepper and clean the seeds out. Place the peppers in the air fryer basket after scooping the mixture into each pepper. 8-10 minutes at 355 degrees, carefully open, and then stir in the cheese.

Step 4. Cook for a another 5 minutes, or until cheese is melted and peppers are just beginning to soften. Then serve.

# Beef Taquitos

**Prep : 15 minutes / Cook Time : 15 minutes / Total Time : 30 mins**

**Servings 20 Taquitos**

## Ingredients

- 453g Ground Beef
- 1 Package Taco Seasoning
- 1 Can of Refried Beans
- 20 White Corn Tortillas
- 85g Shredded Sharp Cheddar

## Directions

Step 1. Start by preparing the ground beef. Brown the meat on medium-high heat and put in the taco seasoning according to the instructions on the packaging.

Step 2. When you are through with the meat, microwave the corn tortillas for about 30 seconds to soften them.

Step 3. Spritz the ninja foodi air fryer basket with non-stick cooking spray or add a piece of paper of foil and spray. Add ground meat, beans, and a touch of cheese to each tortilla.

Step 3. Wrap them firmly and place appear side down in the air fryer. Add a spritz of cooking oil spray, such as olive oil cooking spray. Cook at 390 degrees for 12 minutes and continue with the remaining tortillas.

# Zucchini stuffed with burger

**Prep : 15 minutes / Cook Time : 10 minutes / Total Time : 25 mins**

**Servings 6**

## Ingredients

- 3 Zucchinis
- 340g tomato sauce
- 1 tbsp Italian Seasoning (divide into half)
- 1 Cup Mozzarella, grated

- 453g ground beef
- Salt & Pepper
- 1 tbsp minced Garlic
- Olive Oil Spray

## Directions

Step 1. Wash and dry zucchini gently. Remove the zucchini's stem, then cut each one in half lengthwise. Scrape out the the inside of the zucchini seeds with a spoon to make a boat shape for the ground beef. Lightly season the zucchini with salt and pepper. Add a half-teaspoon of Italian seasoning.

Step 2. Spray the tiny casserole dish that is safe for air frying inside and out. Alternatively, lay zucchini on foil in the air fryer.

Step 3. In a saucepan, cook the ground beef on medium heat with the garlic, ½ tbsp Italian spice, and season with salt and pepper. As beef starts to brown, add the tomato sauce.

Step 4. After thoroughly combining, simmer for a further 3 minutes to fully combine the sauce and beef.

Then, scoop the ground beef into the formed zucchini boats. O n the top of the ground beef add the grated fresh mozzarella.

Step 5. Put the zucchini boats into the ninja foodi air fryer basket or into a small baking dish that will fit into the air fryer. Air fried the zucchini boats at 350°F for 10 minutes. Serve Hot.

# Beef Pizza burgers

**Prep : 10 minutes / Cook Time : 15 minutes / Total Time : 25 mins**

**Servings 4**

## Ingredients

- 453g meatloaf mix ground beef

- 1 Tbsp minced onion

- 43g chopped pepperoni or mini pepperoni slices
- 1 tsp Italian seasoning
- freshly ground black pepper
- 170g sliced mozzarella cheese
- 1 tbsp tomato paste
- ½ tsp salt
- 340g pizza sauce
- 4 crusty round rolls ciabatta rolls

## Directions

Step 1. In a sizable bowl, combine the meatloaf mixture, finely chopped onion, pepperoni, tomato paste, Italian seasoning, salt, and pepper. Mix well until everything is mixed. Split the meat into 4 equal pieces and afterwards shape the burgers, being careful not to over-handle the meat. One nice way to do this is to toss the meat back and forth between your hands like a ball, packing the beef each time you catch it.

Step 2. Compress the balls into patties, making a hole or divot in the center of each patty. As it cooks, this will assist in keeping the burger flat. Cut the rolls in half, then lightly drizzle the cut side with olive oil.

Step 3. Pre-heat the ninja foodi air fryer to 370°F. Air-fry the burger patties for 12-15 minutes, turning them over halfway through the cooking process. Spoon a little pizza sauce on every burger and top with the sliced mozzarella cheese. 3 more minutes of air-frying at 370°F are required to melt the cheese.

Step 4. The burgers should be taken out of the air fryer and left to rest. Place the rolls in the air fryer, cut side up. Air-fry at 380°F for 2 to 3 minutes to toast the rolls.

Step 5. Place the burgers on the toasted rolls after they have rested, top with more Italian seasoning, and serve right away.

# Dijon garlic Lamb Chops

**Prep : 15 minutes / Cook Time : 17 minutes / Total Time : 32 mins**

**Servings 2**

## Ingredients

- 8 pieces of lamb chops
- 8l olive oil
- 1 tsp garlic, minced
- 1 tsp cayenne pepper
- ¼ tsp salt
- 8g Dijon mustard
- 4l soy sauce
- 1 tsp cumin powder
- 1 tsp Italiano spice blend (optional)

## Directions

Step 1. In a medium bowl s tart making the marinade by combining Dijon mustard, olive oil, soy sauce, garlic, cumin powder, cayenne pepper, Italiano spice blend (optional), and salt then mix well.

Step 2. Put lamb chops into a Sealed bag and pour in the marinade. Seal the bag securely after pressing out the air. Squeeze the marinade around the lamb chops to completely coat. Put into the refrigerator and marinade for at least 30 minutes, up to overnight.

Step 3. Put 3 pieces of marinated lamb chops onto a grilling rack on top of the ninja foodi air frying basket, and spread them out equally. Cook the lamb chops for 17 minutes at 350 degrees Fahrenheit, flipping them once halfway through to ensure even cooking.

Step 4. After finishing, let the lamb chops stay in the hot air fryer for an additional five minutes. By doing so, the lamb chops are kept warm and are cooked through while remaining tender. Season with extra salt and cumin, to taste.

# Rack of Lamb with Garlic Aioli

**Prep : 15 minutes / Cook Time : 20 minutes / Total Time : 35 mins**

**Servings 4**

## Ingredients

- One 8-rib rack of lamb (600g)
- Kosher salt and ground black pepper
- 43g cup panko breadcrumbs
- 1 tsp finely chopped fresh thyme
- Nonstick cooking spray, for the air-fryer basket and lamb
- 3 tbsp extra-virgin olive oil
- 43g grated Parmesan
- 1 large clove garlic, grated
- 1 tsp finely chopped fresh rosemary

**Ingredient for Aioli:**

- 6 large cloves garlic (unpeeled)
- 170g mayonnaise
- 2 tsp lemon juice
- Kosher salt and freshly ground black pepper
- 2 tbsp olive oil
- 1 tsp lemon zest plus
- 1 1/2 tsp Worcestershire sauce

## Directions

Step 1. Rack of lamb: Make it possible the rack of lamb to sit at room temperature for 30 minutes prior to actually cooking.

Step 2. Coat the rack of lamb on the both sides with 1 tsp of olive oil, then season with 2 tbsp salt and several pinches of pepper. Set aside on a big plate.

Step 3. In a sizable shallow bowl or pie plate, combine the Parmesan, panko, remaining 2 tablespoons of olive oil, grated garlic, thyme, and rosemary. Add the lamb and tightly press the Parmesan mixture on to meat in an even layer.

Step 4. Unpeeled garlic cloves should be placed on a sheet of aluminum foil with a drizzle of olive oil, a sprinkling of salt, and several grinds of pepper. To create a pouch, fold the foil's sides upward.

Step 5. Spray the basket of a 6-quart air fryer with cooking spray, add the lamb, fat-side up, and the garlic pouch, and preheat the air fryer to 375 degrees F.

Step 6. Apply cooking spray to the lamb's top. Cook the lamb in the air fryer for 18 minutes for medium rare, 20 minutes for medium, and 22 minutes for medium-well, or until the crust is crisp and deeply golden brown and the meat is the desired doneness.

Step 7. Move the lamb to a chopping board, cover loosely with foil and leave to rest for 10 minutes.

Step 8. In the meantime, gently pull the foil packet. Try squeezing out the tender cloves of garlic into the mixing bowl and mash with the olive oil from the bag until smooth. Worcestershire, mayonnaise, and lemon juice should all be combined.

Step 9. Salt and pepper to taste. Set aside.Once a lamb has cooled, slice between both the bones into separate chops and serve hot with the aioli.

# Roast Lamb and Potatoes Air fryer

Prep : 5 minutes / Cook Time : 50 minutes / Total Time : 55 mins
### Servings 4

## Ingredients
**Lamb Ingredients**
- 900 g lamb joint I used half leg
- 1 tbsp fresh rosemary
- 1 tsp dried oregano
- ½ tsp black pepper freshly ground

- 2 garlic cloves sliced
- 1 tbsp olive oil
- ½ tsp coarse sea salt

**For the Potatoes Ingredients**
- 6 medium potatoes cut into wedges
- 1 tsp dried oregano
- 1 tsp salt
- squeeze of lemon

- 1 tbsp olive oil
- 1 tsp garlic granules
- ½ tsp ground black pepper

## Directions

Step 1. Before cooking, take the lamb out of the refrigerator for 30 minutes to let it reach room temperature. It will help it cook fast and evenly.

Step 2. Slice the potatoes into thick wedges and put in a bowl or small dish. Sprinkle with salt, pepper, oregano, and garlic salt before adding a drizzle of olive oil. Add a little lemon juice, combine, and transfer to the Air Fryer's basket.

Step 3. Put the lamb within the same dish and use a sharp knife to make several slits onto the skin. Squeeze small garlic clove slices into the skin. Drizzle with the olive oil and fresh rosemary.

Step 4. Season with salt, pepper and oregano and lay the lamb in the ninja foodi Air Fryer, placing it in another basket of the ninja foodi air fryer.

Step 5. Cook for 8-10 minutes at 200°C (400°F) to create a nice crust. Reduce the heat to 180°C (360°F) and cook for another 30–40 minutes, or until a meat thermometer reads 145°F/63°C for the center of the meat.

Step 6. Test the potatoes are cooked through. The lamb should rest for 20 minutes with a loose cover before serving.

# Lamb Skewers Air fryer

Prep : 15 minutes / Cook Time : 10 minutes / Total Time : 55 mins
### Servings 4

## Ingredients
- 450 g lamb leg
- 15 cm bamboo skewers

- 1/2 onion sliced

**Marinade Ingredients**
- 2 tbsp peanut oil or vegetable oil
- 1 tbsp Shaoxing wine or dry sherry (Optional)

- 2 tbsp light soy sauce (or soy sauce)
- 2 tsp cornstarch

- 2 tsp cumin powder
- 1/2 tsp salt
- 1/4 tsp ground Sichuan peppercorn (or ground black pepper)

- 1/2 tsp chili flakes

## Directions

Step 1. In a small bowl, mix the oil, soy sauce, cornstarch, cumin, chili powder, and salt. Mix well.

Step 2. Cut fat from the lamb meat if needed. Trim the lean portion into 1.5-cm (0.5-inch) pieces. Cut fat into tiny pieces half the size of the lean portions.

Add the lamb and onion into a large bowl.

Step 3. Sprinkle the marinade well over lamb. Mix thoroughly so the lamb is covered equally with the marinade. Marinate for 30 minutes at room temperature or overnight in the refrigerator. Stitch lamb cubes tightly onto skewers, alternating between lean meat and fat bits.

Step 4. Pre-heat the ninja foodi air fryer to 400°F (200°C) when you are ready to cook. Put skewers into the preheated ninja foodi air fryer and air fryer and cook for 7 to 10 minutes, till the scorched on the outside and soft on the inside. Halfway through, flip the lamb skewers and drizzled a generous amount of chili powder and cumin powder across both sides.

# Breaded Zucchini Air fryer

**Prep : 10 minutes / Cook Time : 1 hr / Total Time : 1 hr 10 mins**
**Servings 4**

## Ingredients

- 2 medium zucchini (sliced into 1/4 rounds)
- 96g panko bread crumbs
- 43g freshly grated Parmesan
- 1/4 tsp. garlic powder
- Kosher salt
- Marinara (optional)

- 2 large eggs
- 43g cornmeal
- 1 tsp. dried oregano
- Pinch of crushed red pepper flakes
- Freshly ground black pepper

## Directions

Step 1 . Put zucchini on a sheet lined with towels and pat dry.  In a small bowl, beat eggs, combine oregano, garlic powder, panko, cornmeal, Parmesan, oregano, garlic powder, and red pepper flakes in a separate small bowl. Add salt and black pepper to taste.

Step 2. Work one at a time, drop zucchini rounds into egg, then into panko mixture, squeezing to stick.

Step 3. Working in batches, in a ninja foodi air-fryer basket, organise zucchini in a single layer. Cook at 400°, turning halfway through, till crispy on both sides, about 15- 18 minutes. Serve hot with marinara sauce.

# Air fryer Crispy Avocado Fries

**Prep : 5 minutes / Cook Time : 15 minutes / Total Time : 20 mins**
**Servings 4**

## Ingredients

- 128g Panko breadcrumbs
- 1 tsp. paprika
- 2 large eggs

- 1 tsp. garlic powder
- 136g all-purpose flour
- 2 avocados sliced

## Directions

Step 1. In a small bowl, stir together garlic powder, Panko,  and paprika. Put flour in another small bowl, and in a third small bowl beat eggs.

Step 2 . Slices of avocado should be thoroughly coated after being dipped in flour, egg, and Panko mixture one at a time. Put in ninja foodi air fryer and fry at 400° for 8-10 minuts.

Serve with ranch dressing, if wanted.

# Air fryer Bang Bang Cauliflower

**Prep : 10 minutes / Cook Time : 30 minutes / Total Time : 45 mins**
**Servings 4**

## Ingredients

- 3 tbsp. extra-virgin olive oil
- 1 tbsp. sriracha
- 3 cloves garlic, minced
- kosher salt
- 1 tsp. Chopped cilantro, for garnish
- 2 tbsp. sweet chili sauce
- 1 lime juice
- 1 medium cauliflower (cut into florets)
- Freshly ground black pepper

## Directions

Step 1 . Sriracha, lime juice, Olive oil, sweet chili sauce, and garlic should all be combined in a big bowl.

Step 2. In a bowl a Add cauliflower , season gently with salt and pepper, and mix well.

Step 3. Put one third of the cauliflower in a thin layer in the basket of the ninja foodi Air Fryer. Cook at 360° for 10-12 minutes, turning halfway through.

# Tater Tots

**Prep : 10 minutes / Cook Time : 1hr 40 minutes / Total Time : 1hr 50 mins**
**Servings 4-6**

## Ingredients

- 1.3 kg russet potatoes, peeled
- 1/2 tsp. garlic powder
- Freshly ground black pepper
- 1/2 tsp. kosher salt
- 1/4 tsp. onion powder

## Directions

Step 1. In a big boiling pot of water, add potatoes and boil till the potatoes are met with very little resistance once poked with a knife, approximately 7 minutes, then drain and set aside.

Step 2 . When potatoes are cold enough just to handle, use large holes on a box grater to shred potato. Shredded potatoes, onion powder, salt, garlic powder, and pepper should all be combined in a big bowl. Use your hands to shape approximately 2 tbsp worth of mixture into a tater tot form, gently squishing mixture as required. Use your hands to shape approximately 2 tbsp worth of mixture into a tater tot form, gently squishing mixture as required.

Step 3 . Continuing to work in batches, try placing tater tots in basket of ninja foodi air fryer. Cook on 375° for 18- 20 minutes, pausing to shake basket halfway through, until browned. Take from basket and add salt.

# Air fryer Brussels Sprout Chips

Prep : 5 minutes / Cook Time : 20 minutes / Total Time : 25 mins

Servings 3

## Ingredients

- 226g brussels sprouts, thinly sliced
- 2 tbsp. freshly grated Parmesan (plus more for garnish)
- 1 tsp. garlic powder
- Freshly ground black pepper
- 1 tbsp. extra-virgin olive oil
- Kosher salt
- Caesar dressing, for dipping (optional)

## Directions

Step 1. In a large bowl, combine brussels sprouts along with oil, Parmesan, garlic powder then season with salt and pepper. Organise in an even layer in ninja foodi air fryer.

Step 2. Bake at 350° for 6-8 minutes, mix, and bake 8 minutes more, till crisp and golden.

Step 3. Garnish with much more Parmesan and start serving with caesar dressing for dipping.

# Blooming Onion

Prep : 15 minutes / Cook Time : 30 minutes / Total Time : 45 mins

Servings 4

## Ingredients

**ONION Ingredients**
- 1 large yellow onion
- 128g breadcrumbs
- 1 tsp. kosher salt
- 2 tsp. paprika

**SAUCE Ingredients**
- 227g mayonnaise
- 1/2 tsp. garlic powder
- 1 tsp. horseradish
- Kosher salt

- 3 large eggs
- 1 tsp. onion powder
- 3 tbsp. extra-virgin olive oil
- 1 tsp. garlic powder

- 2 tbsp. ketchup
- 1/4 tsp. dried oregano
- 1/2 tsp. paprika

## Directions

Step 1. Cut the onion's stem off, then place the flat side down. Slice an inch from the base down, into 12 to 16 portions, being cautious not to cut all the way through. Turn over and carefully remove out sections of onion to separate petals.

Step 2. In a small bowl, bowl . stir together eggs and 1 tsp water. In another small bowl, whisk together breadcrumbs and spices. Soak onion into egg wash, after which dredge in breadcrumb mixture, using a ladle to fully coat. Apply oil to the onion.

Step 3. Put in basket of ninja foodi air fryer and cook at 375° till onion is cooked all the way through, 22 to 25 minutes. Sprinkle with more oil as needed.

Step 4. Sauce: In a separate bowl, mix together mayonnaise, ketchup, horseradish, paprika, garlic powder and dried oregano. Add salt to taste. Serve sauce and onions together for dipping.

# Air fryer Cauliflower Tots

**Prep : 10 minutes / Cook Time : 20 minutes / Total Time : 30 mins**
**Servings 6**

## Ingredients

- 512g cauliflower florets steamed
- 85g shredded cheddar
- 85g panko breadcrumbs
- Kosher salt
- 170g ketchup
- Cooking spray
- 1 large egg
- 85g freshly grated Parmesan
- 2 tbsp. freshly chopped chives
- Freshly ground black pepper
- 2 tbsp. Sriracha

## Directions

Step 1. Cut the onion's stem off, then place the flat side down. Slice an inch from the base down, into 12 to 16 portions, being cautious not to cut all the way through. Turn over and carefully remove out sections of onion to separate petals.

Step 2. In a small bowl, bowl . stir together eggs and 1 tsp water. In another small bowl, whisk together breadcrumbs and spices. Soak onion into egg wash, after which dredge in breadcrumb mixture, using a ladle to fully coat. Apply oil to the onion.

Step 3. Put in basket of ninja foodi air fryer and cook at 375° till onion is cooked all the way through, 22 to 25 minutes. Sprinkle with more oil as needed.

Step 4. Sauce: In a separate bowl, mix together mayonnaise, ketchup, horseradish, paprika, garlic powder and dried oregano. Add salt to taste. Serve sauce and onions together for dipping.

# Air fryer salt and pepper tofu

**Prep : 10 minutes / Cook Time : 20 minutes / Total Time : 30 mins**
**Servings 8**

## Ingredients

- 2 tsp vegetable oil
- 1 thinly sliced long red chilli (optional)
- 125ml salt-reduced gluten-free tamari or soy sauce
- 55g caster sugar
- 1 tbsp sea salt flakes
- 1 tsp dried chilli flakes (optional)
- 2-300g Firm tofu (cut into 2cm pieces)
- 1 thinly sliced spring onion
- 1 crushed garlic clove
- 1 tsp sesame oil
- 1 tbsp black peppercorns
- 45g rice flour
- Vegetable oil to drizzle

## Directions

Step 1. Heat the oil in a tiny saucepan over high heat. Add spring onion, sliced chilli, and garlic and cook, stirring, for 1 min or until aromatic. Decrease heat to low. Add sugar and tamari or soy sauce. Cook for 3 minutes or till the sugar melts then by 5 minutes should be sufficient for the sauce to thicken. Stir in sesame oil.

Step 2. Use a mortar and pestle to crush the sea salt, peppercorns, and, if using, the chilli flakes into a fine powder. Put in a separate bowl with the rice flour and mix thoroughly. Then add the tofu to the rice flour mixture and toss it to coat, shaking off excess.

Step 3. Sprinkle oil to a baking tray that will fit to your ninja foodi air fryer at 375°. Cook the tofu, in the duo air fryer basket, turning occasionally, for 5 mins or until golden brown. Move to a plate lined with a clean towel.

Step 4. Organise the tofu on a serving dish. Start serving with the sauce.

# Air fryer breaded mushrooms

**Prep : 10 minutes / Cook Time : 10 minutes / Total Time : 20 mins**
**Servings 4**

## Ingredients

- 2 tbsp plain flour
- 1 tbsp milk
- 200g button mushrooms
- 1 egg
- 75g fried chicken coating mix
- Oil Spray

**Dipping sauce Ingredients**
- 250ml thick Greek yoghurt
- Juice of 1 lemon
- 1 grated cucumber

## Directions

Step 1 . Put flour in a small bowl. Beat egg and milk in a mixing bowl and put coating combination in a third bowl.

Step 2 . Shake off any extra flour before tossing it with the mushrooms. Shake off any excess before adding the coating mixture and tossing to coat with the egg mixture.

Step 3 . Put mushrooms in the ninja foodi air fryer basket and spritz with oil, careful to coat the mushrooms well. Cook for 10 minutes at 200°C, or until golden and thoroughly cooked.

Step 4 . In the meantime, making sauce: Combine all Ingredients in a bowl and adjust seasonings as needed. Serve dipping sauce and mushrooms.

# Vegetable peel crisps

**Prep : 10 minutes / Cook Time : 35 minutes / Total Time : 45 mins**
**Servings 4**

## Ingredients

- Peel of 3 potatoes
- Peel of 1 orange sweet potato

- Peel of 1 orange sweet potato
- Chilli sauce, to serve
- 1 lemon
- 30g sea salt flakes

- Greek yoghurt (optional)
- lemon-herb salt
- 10cm fresh rosemary sprig

## Directions

Step 1. To prepare the lemon-herb salt, use a vegetable peeler to remove strips of rind lengthways from the lemon. Slice each strip in work is divided into two.

Step 2. Put the peel and rosemary inside the basket of ninja foodi air fryer. Cook at 70C for 10 minutes. Take the rosemary out. Cook the peel an additional 10-15 minutes, or until it is dry.

Step 3. Remove and leave aside to cool. Strip dried leaf from the rosemary sprig. Mix dried peel and rosemary leaves in a spice blender or mortar, and grind to a powder. Add to a jar with the salt. Crush and mix gently using the end of a wooden spoon.

Step 4. Wash the vegetable peel and use a clean tea towel to completely dry. Place it in a bowl and drizzle lightly with olive oil then toss to coat. Put in the ninja foodi air fryer's basket in a single layer.

Step5. Cook for 8–10 minutes at 180°C, stirring once or twice, or until dry. Place on a plate. Drizzle with the herb salt to taste. Served with yoghurt and chilli sauce.

# Cauliflower cheese bites

**Prep : 20 minutes / Cook Time : 12 minutes / Total Time : 32 mins**

**Servings 2**

## Ingredients

- 2 eggs
- 40g finely grated parmesan
- 450g florets cauliflower

**Cheesy Sauce Ingredients**

- 20g butter
- 125g sour cream
- 1 green shallot thinly sliced

- 50g panko breadcrumbs
- 2 tsp smokey chipotle seasoning

- 2 finely chopped garlic cloves
- 130g perfect pizza cheese

## Directions

Step 1. Eggs are whisked in a bowl. In a another bowl, mix the breadcrumbs, parmesan, and seasoning. Working in batches, thoroughly coat the cauliflower by dipping it in the egg, followed by the breadcrumb mixture.

Step 2 . Place the crumbed cauliflower in the air fryer's basket. Spray some oil on. Cook, turning and spray coating with oil halfway through cooking, at 180C for 10-12 minutes or till crisp.

Step 3. To start making the cheesy sauce, melt the butter in a small saucepan on a medium-high heat until foamy. Include the garlic. Cook, stirring, for 30 seconds or till aromatic. Mix in the sour cream and cheese. Cook, stirring, for 2-3 minutes or until cheese melts.

Step 4. Place the cheese sauce in a heat proof container.

# Eggplant chips

Prep : 15 minutes / Cook Time : 25 minutes / Total Time : 40 mins

### Servings 4

## Ingredients

- 2 eggs
- 60g panko breadcrumbs
- 2 tsp dried Italian herbs
- 4 eggplants (cut diagonally 7mm slices)
- Tomato pasta sauce (optional)

- 75g plain flour
- 50g finely grated parmesan
- 1/2 tsp ground paprika
- Olive oil cooking spray

## Directions

Step 1. In a small bowl, whisk the eggs barely. In a separate shallow bowl, add the flour. Mix the , parmesan, herbs, breadcrumbs and paprika on a big plate.

Step 2. Put the eggplant slices into the flour, brushing off excess. Continuing to work one at a time, soak eggplant into egg then breadcrumb mixture, pushing firmly to coat.

Step 3. Place half of the eggplant in the air fryer's basket in a single layer. Spray the pan well with oil and cook for 5 minutes at 200 °C. Gently Flip the eggplant and spray again with oil. Cook for an additional five minutes. Place on a plate. Continue with the remaining eggplant.

# Gozleme danish

Prep : 5 minutes / Cook Time : 20 minutes / Total Time : 25 mins

### Servings 2

## Ingredients

- 2 tsp rice bran oil
- 80g frozen spinach (thawed)
- 200g Danish feta (Sliced into half horizontally)
- Lemon wedges (optional)

- ¼ finely chopped medium brown onion
- 1 sheet frozen puff pastry (thawed)
- 1 egg yolk

## Directions

Step 1. A small frying pan with medium-high heat is used to heat the oil. Add the onion and stir for 4–5 minutes, until the onion is golden.Then add the spinach and cook, stirring, for 30 seconds or until combined. Get rid of the heat. Set apart for cooling.

Step 2. The pastry should be put on a sizable cutting board. Place the feta in the centre. Add onion mixture on top. Along the filling's long sides, cut pastry into 2 cm-wide strips by slicing it diagonally.

Step 3. Fold in the short ends. One pastry strip should be folded over the filling before a second, somewhat overlapping strip is added from the other side. Up until everything is enclosed, alternate the strips over the filling. Discard extra pastry or store for subsequent use.

Step 4. Place and brush with egg before using an air fryer. Cook for 15 minutes at 180°C, or until brown and crisp. Make slices of. Start serving with lemon wedges.

# Green Beans with Garlic Air fryer

**Prep : 5 minutes / Cook Time : 10 minutes / Total Time : 15 mins**
**Servings 2**

## Ingredients

- 226g Green Beans
- 1 teaspoon Soy Sauce
- 1 clove Garlic freshly minced
- ¼ teaspoon Black pepper
- Crushed red pepper flakes (optional)

- ½ tablespoon Sesame oil or olive oil
- ¾ teaspoon Rice Vinegar
- ½ teaspoon Ginger freshly grated (optional)
- Sesame Seeds (garnish)

## Directions

Step 1. Clean and cut the rough ends off the green beans then p at them dry.

Step 2. All the spice components should be combined in a sizable bowl and a dd the green beans. Mix them well, so they are fully coated with the spices.

Step 3. Move the seasoned green beans to the ninja foodi air fryer basket. Shake basket to disperse the green beans. Set the ninja foodi air fryer to 380°F.

Step 4. Air fry for 8 minutes for the right texture. Toss the basket half way through.

Step 5. Enjoy green beans after serving them. Alternatively, drizzle some sesame seeds.

# Spaghetti Squash

**Prep : 5 minutes / Cook Time : 25 minutes / Total Time : 30 mins**
**Servings 4**

## Ingredients

- 1 spaghetti squash
- ¼ tsp black pepper

- 2 tsp olive oil
- 2 tbsp parsley

- ¼ tsp salt

## Directions

Step1. Wash the squash thoroughly. Place on cutting board, then trim the ends (stem and bottom). Then split the squash in half through the middle.

Step 2. Scrape out the center seeds with a large spoon to make the mixture clear and clean. Turn the squash over cut the side down, and poked with a fork several times.

Step 3. Put both halves in the ninja foodi air fryer basket cutting side facing up. Sprinkle with olive oil, and rub into the skin. Add salt and pepper to taste.

Baked in the ninja foodi air fryer at 400 degrees F for about 20-25 minutes, or till the flesh easily scrapes off with a fork.

Step 4. Put in a serving bowl. Scrape the squash from the outside in using a fork. Keep going scraping until you've set to release all of the squash on the both sides and you have something that looks like long spaghetti noodles!

Step 5. Garnish with chopped fresh herbs! Any way you want it, serve as a side dish!

# Shrimp Fried Rice

**Prep : 10 minutes / Cook Time :  25 minutes / Total Time : 35 mins**
**Servings 4**

## Ingredients
- 453 g Shrimp (peeled and deveined)
- 1 teaspoon Cornstarch

**For the Rice Ingredients**
- 316 g Cooked Rice
- 25 g Chopped Green Scallions, chopped
- 1 tablespoon soy sauce
- 1 teaspoon pepper

**For the Eggs Ingredients**
- 2 large Eggs
- 1/4 teaspoon pepper

- 1/4 teaspoon pepper

- 140 g Frozen Peas and Carrots, thawed
- 3 tablespoon sesame oil
- 1/2 teaspoon Kosher Salt

- 1/4 teaspoon Kosher Salt

## Directions
Step1. Add cornstarch, salt, and shrimp to a bowl. Place aside.

Step 2. Mix the rice, vegetables, onions, sesame oil, salt, and pepper in a 6 x 3 heatproof pan.

Step 3. Cook for 15 minutes in the ninja foodi Air Fryer at 350 degrees. Shake  the rice halfway through cooking time.

Step 4. Rice should be topped with shrimp, which should be air-fried for five minutes at 350°.

Step 5. While the shrimp cooks whisk the eggs with salt and pepper. Over the shrimp and rice mixture, pour the eggs, and cook for an additional five minutes at 350 degrees.

Step 6. Serve the shrimp and rice after stirring in the eggs.

# Air Fryer  Sriracha Lime Tempeh Bowl

**Prep : 10 minutes / Cook Time :  15 minutes / Total Time : 25 mins**
**Servings 4**

## Ingredients
- 340g tempeh
- 128g fresh corn kernels
- 1 lime juice

- 256g frozen edamame (shelled)
- 2 tbsp sriracha
- 1/2 tsp kosher salt

## Directions
Step1. Your air fryer should be at 400F. Fill a large bowl with the tempeh crumbles. Make sure that each piece fits into a 1x1 cube.

Step 2. Edamame and corn should be added to the tempeh. Combine by tossing.

Toss the mixture once more until it is evenly coated before adding the sriracha, lime juice, and salt.

Step 3. Distributed out the tempeh, edamame and corn evenly in ninja foodi air fryer basket. Don't overfill the basket; if necessary, cook in two batches.

Step 4. Cook at 400F for 10 to 14 minutes. Pull it out when the edamame and tempeh are somewhat browned. After cooling, serve!

# Air Fryer  Crispy roasted lentils

**Prep : 5 minutes / Cook Time :  20 minutes / Total Time : 25 mins**

**Servings 4**

## Ingredients

- 256g cooked lentils canned/fresh
- 1 teaspoon chipotle paste
- 2 tablespoons olive oil

## Directions

Step1. Heating the air fryer to 400 F.In a medium bowl, add the lentils, oil, and chipotle; gently toss to blend. Spread the coated lentils on a small piece of foil, then fold the sides up to form a tray. Depending on how big your air fryer is, you might need to cook these in batches.

Step 2. Roast at 400° F till gently crisp, approximately 15 minutes, stir the mixture halfway through.

# Chickpea Cauliflower Tacos

**Prep : 10 minutes / Cook Time :  20 minutes / Total Time : 30 mins**

**Servings 4**

## Ingredients

- 512g cauliflower florets (Bite size)
- 2 tablespoons olive oil
- 8 small tortillas
- 512g cabbage shredded
- 530g can of chickpeas
- 2 tablespoons taco seasoning (Optional)
- 2 avocados sliced
- coconut yogurt to Sprinkle

## Directions

Step1. Pre-heat ninja foodi air fryer to 390°F/ 200°C. In a large bowl, combine the Chickpeas and cauliflower with the olive oil and taco seasoning then p ut everything into the air fryer's basket.

Step 2. Cook in the air fryer, tossing the basket occasionally, for 20 minutes, or till cooked through. Cauliflower will be golden.    Start serving in tacos with cabbage, avocado slices, and coconut yogurt.

# Black Bean Tostadas

**Prep : 10 minutes / Cook Time :  5 minutes / Total Time : 15 mins**

**Servings 4**

## Ingredients

- Corn tortilla or flour
- olive oil spray

- 128g shredded cheddar cheese
- 2 scallions diced
- 32g sour cream
- 128g diced tomatoes
- 128 black beans, heated
- other toppings (lime, guacamole etc)

## Directions

Step1. Begin by laying the tortillas out in the ninja foodi air fryer basket. They should be liberally sprayed with olive oil before being air-fried for three minutes on each side at 400 degrees F.

Step 2. Top with cheddar cheese and continue to air fry for an additional one to three minutes or until the cheese is melted. (Air fryer still set at 400 degrees Fahrenheit)

Step 3. Add extra cheddar cheese, black beans, diced tomatoes, and onions to the top. On top, I sprinkled some sour cream.

Enjoy! Plate and serve!

# Green Beans with Pesto

**Prep : 10 minutes / Cook Time : 8 minutes / Total Time : 18 mins**
**Servings 4**

## Ingredients

- 453g green beans
- 170g fresh basil
- lemon zest
- 1/2 teaspoon sea salt
- 5 Tablespoons Olive Oil
- 32g walnuts
- 512g fresh arugula; divided
- 1 clove garlic; roughly chopped
- 85g Parmesan cheese (finely grated)

## Directions

Step1. Clean and cut the green beans. Place in a big bowl and sprinkle with olive oil. Salt and pepper to taste then toss to coat.

Step 2. In a food processor dish, place the walnuts, baby arugula, sea salt, basil, lemon zest and juice. Process the items combined until they are finely chopped.

Step 3. Process the items combined until they are finely chopped.

With the lid open, drizzle in 4-6 tablespoons olive oil.

Step 4. Preheat ninja foodi air fryer to 375 F. Cook green beans for 8 minutes at 375 degrees. Shake the basket halfway through the overall Cook Time.

Step 5. Take beans from the ninja foodi air fryer and put back in the big bowl then a dd 2 tablespoons pesto and toss to combine.

Step 6. Arrange beans on a dish and garnish with remaining baby arugula. Finish adding it with Parmesan cheese. Serve.

# Crispy Black-Eyed Peas

**Prep : 5 minutes / Cook Time : 10 minutes / Total Time : 15 mins**
**Servings 6**

## Ingredients

- 425 g can black-eyed peas
- 1/4 tsp salt optional
- 1/8 tsp black pepper
- 1/2 tsp chili powder
- 1/8 tsp chipotle chili powder
- 1/8 tsp smoked salt

## Directions

Step1. Using a colander or sieve, drain the juice out from black-eyed peas. Carefully rinse them off under running clean water and let them dry up for a few minutes. Spread them out on a platter and remove any mashed or mushy peas.

Step 2. Mix together the spice Ingredients and apply whatever amount you like over the peas, carefully tossing the peas to make sure all are covered.  Preheat your ninja foodi air fryer to 350-360 F. Place the peas in the basket and air fry for 3-5 minutes.

Step 3. Take the basket and shake or swirl to redistribute the peas. Air fried for a further 5 minutes or till peas were crunchy on the outside and slightly soft on the inside. Cool down and serve immediately.

# Crispy Black-Eyed Peas

**Prep : 10 minutes / Cook Time :  10 minutes / Total Time : 20 mins**
**Servings 8**

## Ingredients

- 2 pieces bacon diced
- 128g corn, drained
- 2 tablespoons minced onion
- 1 teaspoon salt
- 1/2 teaspoon basil dried
- 2 teaspoons olive oil
- 128g lima beans, drained
- 64g diced toamtoes, drained
- 1/2 teaspoon black pepper

## Directions

Step1. Combine the diced bacon, onions, salt, black pepper, lima beans, tomatoes, corn,  and basil in a large bowl. Mix well.

Step 2. Mix with salt, black pepper, olive oil, and dried basil. Mix thoroughly, covering the vegetables well. Pour into a baking dish.  Set the ninja foodi air fryer to 380 degrees F, air fryer set for 8 to 10 minutes. Mix the succotash regularly. Enjoy! Plate and serve!

# Lentil Patties

**Prep : 5 minutes / Cook Time :  20 minutes / Total Time : 25 mins**
**Servings 5**

## Ingredients

- 512g cooked brown/green lentils
- 1 tsp garlic powder
- 1 tsp smoked paprika
- 68g cup oat flour
- 1 tsp cumin powder
- 1/2 tsp chili powder

- 1/2 tsp liquid smoke
- 21g cup chopped parsley
- 21g chopped cilantro
- salt to taste

## Directions

Step 1. If using canned lentils, skip this step. If using dry green/brown lentils, pressure cook it in instant pot for 5 minutes with 1 liter of water, some garlic powder and salt per taste. Release pressure and keep aside to cool.

Step 2. In a huge bowl, mix all your Ingredients and stir thoroughly. Use your hands to shape patties. Lightly spray ninja foodi air fryer with neutral oil to avoid patties from sticking. Air fry at 400 F for 20 minutes, be sure to flip half way through. Ensure to line your baking tray with a non-stickstick silicone mat or parchment paper.

Step 3. Once ready, whether enjoy them fresh with Vegan Cheese sauce, and some pickled red onion on top as an appetizer or keep them in the refrigerator once cooled to use throughout the week.

# Cannellini Beans Air fried

**Prep : 5 minutes / Cook Time :  15 minutes / Total Time : 20 mins**
**Servings 6**

## Ingredients

- 25gcannellini beans
- 1 teaspoon seasoning any type
- 2 teaspoons olive oil

## Directions

Step 1. Use a colander to drain the cannellini beans, then rinse them with cold water. After that, spread them out on a kitchen towel or paper towel to dry for about 10 minutes.

Step 2. In a sizable bowl, combine the cannellini beans with the oil, salt, and pepper, and toss to coat.

Step 3. Put the beans in the ninja foodi air fryer basket, preheat to 400 degrees Fahrenheit, and cook for 12 to 15 minutes, shaking the basket occasionally. When the beans are crispy, remove!

# Cheesy White Bean-Tomato Air fried

**Prep : 5 minutes / Cook Time :  10 minutes / Total Time : 15 mins**
**Servings 4**

## Ingredients

- 60l extra-virgin olive oil
- 3 tablespoons tomato paste
- 30ml boiling water
- 151g mozzarella (coarsely grated)
- 3 fat garlic cloves, thinly sliced
- 2 (425g) cans white beans
- Kosher salt and black pepper

## Directions

Step 1. Oven temperature set to 475 degrees. Heat the olive oil in a 10-inch ovenproof tin over medium-high heat. Fry the garlic for about a minute, or until it turns light golden. To avoid splattering, stir in the tomato paste and fry for 30 seconds, lowering the heat as necessary to keep the garlic from burning.

Step 2. Stir together the beans, water, and ample amounts of salt and pepper. Sprinkle the cheese evenly over the top, then put it in the air fryer for 5 to 10 minutes, or till the cheese has melted and started to turn golden. Run the skillet under the broiler for a minute or two if the top isn't as toasted as you'd like it to be. Serve right away.

# Edamame Air fried

**Prep : 2 minutes / Cook Time :  12 minutes / Total Time : 14 mins**
**Servings 5**

## Ingredients

- 450g Frozen Edamame
- 1 tbsp Lemon Juice
- 1 tbsp Vegetable Oil
- 1 tsp Sea Salt

## Directions

Step 1. Add the vegetable oil to the edamame and toss. It should be placed in the air fryer's basket.

Step 2. For six minutes, air fry the edamame at 400 degrees Fahrenheit.

Step 3. To rearrange the edamame in the basket, turn on the air fryer. For a further 6 minutes, air fried at 400 degrees F.

Step 4. Edamame should be poured into a fresh bowl. Add sea salt and lemon juice before tossing. Serve.

# Baked Beans Air fried

**Prep : 10 minutes / Cook Time :  20 minutes / Total Time : 30 mins**
**Servings 4**

## Ingredients

- 790g baked beans any flavor
- 21g bacon diced, and cooked
- 85g cup ketchup
- 1 tablespoon Worcestershire sauce
- 1 tablespoon honey
- 21g onions diced, and cooked
- 55g cup brown sugar
- 1 tablespoon mustard yellow
- 1 tablespoon apple cider vinegar

## Directions

Step 1. All of the Ingredients should be combined and thoroughly mixed in a big basin. The beans should be put in a little casserole dish (this must be oven safe)

Step 2. Set the air fryer to the air fryer setting, place the casserole dish in the basket, and cook it at 380 degrees F while stirring frequently. Set 15 to 20 minutes in advance.

# Broccoli Quinoa Salad

**Prep : 10 minutes / Cook Time :  20 minutes / Total Time : 30 mins**

## Ingredients

- 1 bag Success® Tri-Color Quinoa
- 2 tbsp olive oil
- 1 can (500g) chickpeas
- 43g basil pesto
- 85l lemon juice
- 1 head broccoli
- 1/4 tsp salt
- 128g jarred roasted red peppers sliced
- 1 tbsp lemon zest

## Directions

Step 1 . Follow the Directions on the quinoa package to prepare it. Cut florets into small pieces after separating from stem. Trim the tough end of the broccoli stem and throw it away. Peel and chop the remaining stem into bite-sized pieces. Combine the florets, chopped stems, oil, and salt in a medium bowl.

Step 2. Preheat ninja foodi at air-fryer. Put the broccoli in the air fryer basket in batches. Cook for five to seven minutes at 400°F, or until golden, crispy, and tender.

Step 3. chickpeas, roasted red peppers, Quinoa, air-fried broccoli, pesto, lemon zest, and lemon juice should all be thoroughly blended in a big bowl.

# Air fryer Barley, Mushroom and Sweet Potato Risotto

**Prep : 10 minutes / Cook Time : 20 minutes / Total Time : 30 mins**
**Servings 4**

## Ingredients

- 2 onions (medium chopped)
- 3 tbsp oil
- 1 kg sweet potatoes (peeled and diced)
- 225 g can mushrooms
- 100 ml skim milk
- 1 teaspoon tarragon dried
- 2 cloves garlic (chopped)
- 1.25 litres stock
- 350 g pearl barley
- 4 tbsp parmesan cheese
- 1 teaspoon thyme dried

## Directions

Step 1. In a big saucepan, bring the stock to a rolling boil.

Step 2. In a Ninja Foodi air fryer pan, combine the chopped sweet potatoes with 2 tablespoons of oil or 1 tablespoon of duck fat. Cook for 10 minutes, then add the onion, garlic, and barley. Cook for another 5 minutes. At this point, add 4 cups of extremely hot stock all at once. Cook for 30 minutes.

Step 3. After 30 minutes, use the cup of stock you set aside to modify the consistency to your liking, add the tinned mushrooms, milk, parmesan cheese, and herbs, cook for a further 5 to 7 minutes, and then serve immediately.

## Cheese bread puffs Air fried

Prep : 20 minutes / Cook Time :  1h 15 minutes / Total Time : 1h 35 mins

makes 30

### Ingredients

- 250ml milk
- 300g tapioca flour
- 70g finely grated parmesan cheese
- 125ml vegetable oil
- 2 eggs

### Directions

Step 1 . For 2 minutes, or until the milk simmers, boil the milk and oil in a saucepan over medium heat. Stir in the flour after adding it. Add the Ingredients to a stand mixer's bowl. 2 minutes, or until smooth and slightly cooled, should be beat.

Step 2 . One at a time, add the eggs beat  properly after each addition. Add the cheese and mix just until incorporated. Shape tablespoons of batter into balls using wet hands.

Step 3 . Trim the baking paper to fit the base of the air fryer basket. On the baking paper, distribute the balls 5 cm apart. Cook for 15 minutes at 180°C, or until golden and puffy. Continue with the remaining balls. Serve.

## Mozzarella chips Air fried

Prep : 20 minutes / Cook Time :  5 minutes / Total Time : 25 mins

Serves  8

### Ingredients

- 2 eggs
- 3 tsp garlic powder
- 32g cornflake crumbs550g block mozzarella
- Creamy avocado dipping sauce (optional)
- 78ml lemon juice
- 2 tbsp basil pesto
- 2 tbsp plain flour
- 85g panko breadcrumbs
- Olive oil spray
- 1 avocado (roughly chopped)
- 85g plain Greek-style yoghurt
- 1 green onion (roughly chopped)

### Directions

Step 1. In a small food processor, combine the avocado, juice, yoghurt, pesto, and onion to make the creamy avocado dipping sauce. Add salt and pepper to taste. Process until blended and smooth. Place in a basin. Cover. Keep chilled until needed.

Step 2. Place baking paper on a sizable tray. Place . In a small bowl, mix the flour and garlic powder. Use salt to season. In a separate shallow bowl, whisk the eggs. In a bowl, combine the breadcrumbs.

Step 3. Slice the mozzarella cheese into sticks that are 2 cm long. To coat cheese, dip it in flour. Shake off any extra. Sticks should be covered with breadcrumbs and egg mixture in batches. Put on the prepared tray. Freeze for a full hour, or until solid.

Step 4. Spray a lot of oil on the mozzarella sticks. baking paper within the ninja foodi air fryer basket

# Garlic Bread Air fried

**Prep : 5 minutes / Cook Time : 5 minutes / Total Time : 10 mins**
**Serves 8**

## Ingredients

- 57g butter (softened)
- 2 garlic cloves minced
- 8 slices French or ciabatta bread
- 3 tablespoons grated Parmesan cheese
- 2 teaspoons minced fresh parsley

## Directions

Step 1. Set the nina foodi air fryer to 350 degrees. Spread over bread after combining the first 4 Ingredients in a small bowl.

Step 2. Place the bread on the tray in the air fryer basket in batches. Cook bread for 3 minutes or till golden brown. Serve hot.

# Garlic Bread Air fried

**Prep : 5 minutes / Cook Time : 10 minutes / Total Time : 15 mins**
**Serves 2**

## Ingredients

- Corn tortillas
- Cooking spray
- Salt

## Directions

Step 1. For a modest quantity intended for 1-2 people, 4 tortillas are more than enough to begin with. To make triangles, stack tortillas on top of one another and slice them once horizontally and once vertically.

Step 2. Place the tortilla pieces in a single layer in the air fryer basket. Work may need to be done in batches.

Step 3. Sprinkle salt over each tortilla slice after liberally sprinkling frying oil over them. If you don't really have cooking spray, you can simply brush some oil on each slice.

Step 4. Turn on the ninja foodi air fryer and cook for 8–10 minutes at 350°F. Watch your chips carefully since some will finish cooking sooner than the 8-minute mark while others will take the entire 10 minutes to crisp up.

Step 5. Remove the crispy tortilla chips from the air fryer and serve them with homemade pico de gallo or pre-made salsa.

# Frozen Corn dog Air fried

**Prep : 2 minutes / Cook Time : 2 minutes / Total Time : 4 mins**

**Serves 3**

## Ingredients

• 1 package frozen corn dogs

## Directions

Step 1. Your ninja foodi air fryer needs two minutes of 400°F heating. Then place a single layer of frozen corn dogs in the basket and bake for eight minutes.

Step 2. With tiny bowls of ketchup, mustard, barbecue sauce, or other condiments for dipping, serve your air-fried corn dogs. Your air fryer needs two minutes of 400° F heating.

# Buffalo Bites Air fried

**Prep : 10 minutes / Cook Time : 30 minutes / Total Time : 40 mins**

**Serves 6**

## Ingredients

• 1 small head florets cauliflower

• 3 tablespoons Buffalo wing sauce

• 2 tablespoons olive oil

• 3 tablespoons butter

## Dip Ingredients

• 160g 2% cottage cheese

• 21g crumbled blue cheese

• Celery sticks (optional)

• 85 fat-free plain Greek yogurt

• 1 envelope ranch salad dressing mix

## Directions

Step 1. Set the ninja foodi air fryer to 350 degrees. Cauliflower and oil are combined in a big basin and mixed to coat. Cauliflower should be placed in the air fryer basket in single layers in batches. Cook for 10-15 minutes, stirring halfway through, or until the edges are browned and the florets are soft.

Step 2. Buffalo sauce and melted butter should be mixed together in a big basin. Cauliflower is added; it is coated. the serving platter after transfer. Mix the Ingredients for the dip in a small bowl. Serve with celery sticks and cauliflower, if desired.

# Fig and Goat Cheese meatballs

**Prep : 45 minutes / Cook Time : 25 minutes / Total Time : 1 hr 10 mins**

**makes 1 dozen**

## Ingredients

• 28 g panko bread crumbs

• 1 large egg

- 453g bulk Italian sausage
- 118g red wine vinegar
- 1 cinnamon stick (3 inches)
- 1 whole star anise
- 1/2 cup water
- 56g fresh goat cheese
- 55g sugar
- 2 whole cloves
- 1/2 cup dried figs (chopped)
- Chopped fresh chives, optional

## Directions

Step 1. In your ninja foodi air fryer set it to 350 degrees. Combine bread crumbs and egg in a big bowl. Add the sausage and stir just enough to combine. Make 18 equal Servings.

Step 2. To completely enclose 1/2 teaspoon of cheese, mold each serving. Place meatballs in the air fryer basket in batches on a greased surface. Cook for 25–30 minutes, or until well cooked.

Step 3. While this is going on, heat up the vinegar, sugar, cinnamon, cloves, and star anise in a big pot. Simmer for five minutes on low heat. Throw away the star anise, cloves, and cinnamon. Add the figs and simmer for 8 to 10 minutes, until soft.

Step 4. Remove from heat and let cool a little. Place in a blender. Process the addition of 1/2 cup water until virtually smooth. accompany with meatballs. Add chopped chives to the meatballs' tops, if you want.

# Beef Wellington Wontons

**Prep : 35 minutes / Cook Time : 10 minutes / Total Time : 45 mins**
**makes 3 dozen**

## Ingredients

- 225g lean ground beef (90% lean)
- 1 tablespoon olive oil
- 128g teaspoons chopped shallot
- 1 cup each chopped fresh baby portobello, shiitake and white mushrooms
- 60ml dry red wine
- 1/2 teaspoon salt
- 1 package (340g) wonton wrappers
- 1 tablespoon water
- 1 tablespoon butter
- 2 garlic cloves, minced
- 1 tablespoon minced fresh parsley
- 1/4 teaspoon pepper
- 1 large egg
- Cooking spray

## Directions

Step 1. Set air fryer to 325 degrees. Cook and shred the beef in a small skillet over medium heat for 4–5 minutes or until it is no longer pink.

Step 2. Place in a large bowl. Butter and olive oil are heated over medium-high heat in the same skillet. Cook the shallot and garlic for one minute. Wine and mushrooms are combined.

Step 3. Add to beef after cooking mushrooms for 8 to 10 minutes until they are soft. Add parsley, salt, and pepper, and stir.

Step 4. Fill the middle of each wonton wrapper with approximately 2 tablespoons of filling. Combine water and egg. Apply egg mixture to wonton edges, fold opposite corners over filling, and press to seal.

Step 5. Wontons should be arranged in a single layer on a greased tray in the air fryer basket and sprayed with cooking spray in batches.

Step 6. Cook for 4-5 minutes, or until gently browned. Toss with cooking spray and turn. Cook for an additional 4-5 minutes, or until crisp and golden. Serve hot.

# Tortellini with Prosciutto

### Prep : 25 minutes / Cook Time : 10 minutes / Total Time : 45 mins
### makes 3 dozen

## Ingredients

- 1 tablespoon olive oil
- 4 garlic cloves coarsely chopped
- 1 tablespoon minced fresh basil
- 1/4 teaspoon pepper

- 3 tablespoons finely chopped onion
- 1 can (425g) tomato puree
- 1/4 teaspoon salt

## tortellini Ingredients:

- 2 large eggs
- 85g seasoned bread crumbs
- 2 tablespoons grated pecorino Romano cheese
- 1/2 teaspoon salt
- 1 package (425g) refrigerated prosciutto ricotta tortellini

- 2 tablespoons 2% milk
- 1 teaspoon garlic powder
- 1 tablespoon minced fresh parsley
- Cooking spray

## Directions

Step 1. Oil should be heated in a small pan over medium-high heat. Stir and sauté the onion and garlic for 3 to 4 minutes, or until they are soft.

Step 2. Add the salt, pepper, and tomato puree after stirring. Boiling over; turn down the heat. 10 minutes of covered simmering. Stay warm. Heat the air fryer to 350 degrees in the interim.

Step 3. Combine the milk and eggs in a small bowl. Bread crumbs, cheese, parsley, salt, and garlic powder should all be combined in a separate bowl.

Step 4. Tortellini is dipped in egg mixture, then is coated in bread crumbs. Tortellini should be placed in a single layer on a greased tray in the air fryer basket and sprayed with cooking spray.

Tep 5. Cook for 4-5 minutes, or until golden brown. Toss with cooking spray and turn. Cook for another 4-5 minutes, or until golden brown. Serve with sauce and top with more fresh basil, minced.

# Turkey Croquettes

### Prep : 20 minutes / Cook Time : 10 minutes / Total Time : 45 mins
### Serves  6

## Ingredients

- 450g mashed potatoes with added milk and butter
- 68g shredded Swiss cheese
- 2 teaspoons minced fresh rosemary
- 1/2 teaspoon salt
- 384g finely chopped cooked turkey
- 2 tablespoons water
- Butter-flavored cooking spray
- 68g grated Parmesan cheese
- 1 shallot finely chopped
- 1 teaspoon minced fresh sage
- 1/4 teaspoon pepper
- 1 large egg
- 21g panko bread crumbs
- Sour cream (optional)

## Directions

Step 1. the air fryer to 350 degrees. Mash potatoes with cheeses, shallot, rosemary, sage, salt, and pepper in a large bowl; stir in turkey. Lightly but thoroughly combine.

Step 2. Form into twelve patties that are 1 inch thick.Egg and water should be whisked in a small bowl. Another small bowl should be filled with bread crumbs. Croquettes should be dipped in egg mixture, then coated with bread crumbs by patting them down.

Step 3. Croquettes should be placed in a single layer on a greased tray in the air fryer basket and sprayed with cooking spray as you go. Cook for 4-5 minutes, or until golden brown. Toss with cooking spray and turn. Cook for 4-5 minutes, or until golden

# Rosemary Sausage Meatballs

### Prep : 20 minutes / Cook Time : 10 minutes / Total Time : 30 mins
### Makes 2 dozen

## Ingredients

- 4 garlic cloves, minced
- 2 tablespoons olive oil
- 1 jar (113g) diced pimientos, drained
- 21g cup minced fresh parsley
- 900g bulk pork sausage
- 1 teaspoon curry powder
- 1 large egg, lightly beaten
- 21g  dry bread crumbs
- 1 tablespoon minced fresh rosemary
- Pretzel sticks (optional)

## Directions

Step 1. In the ninja foodi air fryer set to 400 degrees. Heat oil in a small skillet over medium heat. Sauté curry powder and garlic until fragrant, about 1-2 minutes. Cool a little.

Step 2. Egg, pimientos, bread crumbs, parsley, rosemary, and garlic mixture should all be combined in a basin. Add the sausage and stir just enough to combine.

Step 3. Create a 1-1/4" form. balls. Place on tray in air fryer basket in a single layer; fry for 7–10 minutes, or until lightly browned and cooked through. Serve alongside pretzels if preferred.

# Pasta Chips Air fried

### Prep : 20 minutes / Cook Time : 10 minutes / Total Time : 30 mins
### Makes 2 dozen

## Ingredients

- 250g farfalle pasta
- 43g grated Parmesan cheese
- 1 teaspoon Italian seasoning
- 1 tablespoon olive oil
- 1 teaspoon garlic powder
- ½ teaspoon salt

## Directions

Step 1. In a large pot of lightly salted water should come to a boil before adding the pasta, which should be cooked for around 8 minutes while stirring occasionally. Rinse not, drain not. Give it two minutes to sit.

Step 2. Achieve a 400°F air fryer temperature (200 degrees C).

Step 3. While this is going on, add the pasta to a large bowl, drizzle with olive oil, and add the Parmesan, garlic powder, Italian seasoning, and salt. Stir to incorporate well. In the air fryer basket, arrange 1/4 of the pasta in a single layer.

Step 3. Cook for 5 minutes in the preheated air fryer, then turn and cook for an additional 2 to 3 minutes. Any pasta chips that have clumped together should be broken apart and transferred to a plate lined with paper towels to cool entirely. Continue with remaining pasta.

# Everything bagel Bites

**Prep : 20 minutes / Cook Time : 10 minutes / Additional Time:10 mins / Total Time : 40 mins**

Serves 8

## Ingredients

- 136g all-purpose flour
- ½ teaspoon salt
- 57g garlic and herb cheese spread
- 2 teaspoons everything bagel seasoning
- 2 teaspoons baking powder
- 30g fat-free Greek yogurt
- 1 large egg white
- cooking spray

## Directions

Step 1. Heat the air fryer to 330 degrees Fahrenheit (165 degrees C). Cooking spray the air fryer basket, then set it aside.

Step 2. In a bowl, combine the flour, salt, and baking powder. Yogurt should be added and thoroughly mixed with a fork.

Step 3. Add flour to the work surface. Take the dough out of the bowl and knead it about 12 times, or until it is no longer sticky. If more flour is required, add a little more.

Step 4. Divide the dough into 8 equal pieces, then use your palm to flatten each piece into a circle. Each circle should have a 1/2 tablespoon of cheese put in the middle. Roll the dough into a ball, covering the cheese with the edges pulled up, and pinch the seams shut.

Step 5. Every piece of bagel is brushed with egg white, then bagel seasoning is added.

Step 6. Place the bagels in the air fryer basket by placing the seam sides down. Don't crowd the area. You might need to cook the food in two batches depending on the size of your air fryer.

Step 7. 10–12 minutes, till browned in the air fryer. Bites of bagels should be removed from the basket and allowed to cool for ten minutes before serving.

## Whole Duck Air fryer

**Prep : 10 minutes / Cook Time : 45 minutes / Total Time :  55 mins**

**Serves  4**

### Ingredients

- 1 whole duck (350g)
- 1 tablespoon rosemary chopped
- ½ teaspoon salt
- 1 teaspoon garlic minced
- 2 tablespoons olive oil
- 1 teaspoon thyme
- ½ teaspoon black pepper

### Directions

Step 1. If you're starting with a frozen duck, allow it to defrost for 24 to 48 hours in the fridge. Remove the neck and any internal giblets after the duck has defrosted.

Step 2. Rinse, then use paper towels to pat dry. Wait to season the duck until it is ready.

Step 3. All of the seasonings should be combined in a small mixing basin. Apply a thin layer of olive oil all over the duck before seasoning.

Step 4. Transfer the duck to the air fryer basket with the breast facing up, and air fried for 45 to 55 minutes at 300 degrees Fahrenheit.

Step 5. The legs must be able to move freely during cooking in order for the duck's juices and fat to drain.

Step 6. The thickest section of the duck's breast should be 170 degrees Fahrenheit inside.

Step 7. Allow the duck to rest for about 10 minutes after it reaches that temperature before cutting.

## Bacon wrap scallops

**Prep : 5 minutes / Cook Time : 20 minutes / Total Time :  25 mins**

**Serves  4**

### Ingredients

- 16 large sea scallops (Pat try)
- 16 toothpicks
- freshly ground black pepper
- 8 slices cut bacon
- olive oil spray

### Directions

Step 1. the air fryer for three minutes @ 400F. Put the bacon in the air fryer and cook for three minutes, flipping halfway through. Take out and cool on a paper towel.

Step 2. The scallops' side muscles should be removed. To eliminate any moisture, pat the scallops dry with paper towels.

Step 3. Each scallop should be wrapped in a piece of bacon and fastened with a toothpick.

Step 4. Scallops should be lightly seasoned with black pepper and olive oil.

In the air fryer, arrange the scallops in a single layer and cook them for 8 minutes, flipping them over halfway through, until they are soft and opaque. Serve warm.

# Baked Brie

**Prep : 10 minutes / Cook Time : 15 minutes / Total Time :  25 mins**
**Serves  8**

## Ingredients

- 1 sheet puff pastry (thawed)
- 128g fruit preserves
- 1 egg
- 226g brie cheese
- 2 Tbsp. toasted nuts
- 1 Tbsp. water

## Directions

Step 1. set the air fryer to 375 degrees.The puff pastry is unfolded. On the pastry sheet's center, place the brie. Don't remove the cheese's rind.

Step 2. Add the preserves and nuts on top of the brie.

Step 3. Gather the dough corners at the top and bring them up and over the brie. To seal the pastry's edges, tightly pinch them together.

Step 4. Mix the egg and water together in a mixing bowl. An uniform layer of egg should be brushed onto the pastry.

Step 5. Transfer the brie with care to the basket. For 15-20 minutes, air fried the brie at 375°F, or until the pastry is golden brown and somewhat puffy.

Step 6. Before taking the brie from the air fryer and serving, let it to cool for five minutes.

# Salami and Cheese Egg Rolls

**Prep : 5 minutes / Cook Time : 7 minutes / Total Time :  12 mins**
**Serves  2**

## Ingredients

- 6 egg roll wrappers
- 6 pieces of string cheese
- marinara for dipping (Optional)
- 12 slices genoa salami
- kosher salt

## Directions

Step 1. On an egg roll wrapper, place two pieces of salami, gently overlapping one another. After placing a piece of string cheese on top of the salami, wrap the ends of the cheese in the salami.

Step 2. Place the cheese and salami sandwich close to the bottom-left corner of the egg roll wrapper. To cover the cheese, carefully fold the sides of the wrapper toward the center, taking careful not to damage it.

Step 3. Roll up halfway. Before rolling the wrapper all the way up, wet your finger and sketch around the corners with it. The final wet corner should be rolled around the mozzarella stick. Repeat with the remaining cheese and wrappers.

Step 4. Spray the air fryer with olive oil spray and add six mozzarella sticks. Add some kosher salt.

Step 5. After flipping, cooking for a further 3 minutes at 350 degrees while spraying the other side with olive oil spray and kosher salt. If preferred, serve with mustard or marinara sauce for dipping.

# Sweet and spicy Apricot Glazed Chicken Drumsticks

**Prep : 15 minutes / Cook Time : 22 minutes / Total Time :  37 mins**

**Serves  2**

## Ingredients

- 4 to 6 chicken drumsticks
- ½ tsp pepper

**Glaze Ingredients**

- 64g apricot preserves
- 1/4 tsp chili powder

- 1 tsp salt
- ½ tsp seasoned salt

- 2 tsp Dijon mustard
- 1/2 tsp soy sauce

## Directions

Step 1. For the Glaze. In a small saucepan, add the apricot preserves, mustard, chili powder, and soy sauce. Whisk to incorporate. Heat for 5 to 10 minutes on low heat until just slightly thickened. Heat has been removed; set aside.

Step 2. Spray some olive oil on the chicken and the air fryer basket. In a small bowl, mix the salt, pepper, and seasoning salt.

Step 3. Chicken should be placed in the air fryer basket with half the seasoning mixture sprinkled on top.

Step 4. Cook for 10 minutes at 370 degrees. Flip chicken after removing it. Sprinkle the remaining Ingredients on top after applying more olive oil.

Step 5. Reposition the chicken in the air fryer and cook for another ten minutes.

Chicken should be removed, sauced, and cooked an additional 2 minutes.

# Creamed Corn Casserole

**Prep : 5 minutes / Cook Time : 45 minutes / Total Time :  50 mins**

**Serves  6**

## Ingredients

- 133g butter melted
- 73g sugar
- ½ t garlic salt
- 1 can corn drained

- 34g AP flour
- 2 eggs beaten
- 170g milk (dairy or non-dairy)
- 1 can creamed corn

## Directions

Step 1. Melted butter and flour should be combined in a medium-sized bowl. Blend the two Ingredients in a whisk until smooth.

Step 2. Add the milk, sugar, and beaten eggs. Combine by whisking. Add the creamed corn, whole kernal corn that has been rinsed, and garlic salt. To blend, stir.

Step 3. Put the mixture in a basin that can be baked. Place that bowl on the air fryer tray or in the basket. At 320F/160C, air fried for 40–45 minutes. Enjoy the dish when it has rested for ten minutes.

# Strawberry Oatmeal

**Prep : 10 minutes / Cook Time : 10 minutes / Total Time : 20 mins**
**Serves 4**

## Ingredients

- 236ml of milk
- 256g of strawberries, diced
- 1/2 teaspoon of baking powder
- 1/3 teaspoon of salt
- 16g of slivered almonds
- 1 egg
- 85g of rolled oats
- 1/2 teaspoon of ground cinnamon
- 50g of brown sugar

## Directions

Step 1. Mix the milk and egg first. Mix well. Oatmeal, brown sugar, salt, baking powder, and cinnamon should all be thoroughly combined in a separate basin.

Apply olive oil spray to a pan that is safe for air frying.

Step 2. Next, layer the oatmeal mixes with 1/4 cup of the diced strawberries on the bottom, followed by the egg/milk combination.

Step 3. Observe for ten minutes. Then top that with more strawberries. Add nutmeg and almonds to the top.

Step 4. You should place the pan in your air fryer and set the temperature for 10 minutes at 320 degrees F. After ten minutes, check in to see how it's doing.

after it is finished. Before serving, take the food out of the air fryer and let it sit for a while. It will.

# Ham and Potato Casserole

**Prep : 5 minutes / Cook Time : 25 minutes / Total Time : 30 mins**
**Serves 6**

## Ingredients

- 1 can condensed cream of mushroom soup (295g)
- ¼ teaspoon salt
- 453g small red potatoes (cut in half)
- 256g cooked ham diced
- 118ml milk
- ¼ teaspoon pepper
- 64g onion diced

## Directions

Step 1. Mix the cream of mushroom soup, milk, salt, and pepper in a medium bowl.

Step 2. Add the sliced potatoes, diced ham, onion, and one cup of cheese after stirring until the mixture forms a creamy sauce.

Step 3. Put the Ingredients in a baking dish that will fit in your air fryer after they have been thoroughly blended.

Step 4. Until potatoes are tender, air fried at 400° Fahrenheit for 20 to 25 minutes. At least twice or three times during cooking, stir the casserole.

Step 5. When the potatoes are tender, top the casserole with shredded cheddar or swiss cheese. Put the casserole back in the air fryer and cook it for an additional few minutes, or until the cheese is melted. Optional (Add some cheese, cooked stuffing, or dried onions as a garnish.)

# Cob loaf dip

**Prep : 35 minutes / Cook Time : 30 minutes / Total Time :  1 hr 5 mins**
**Serves  8**

## Ingredients

- 450g cob loaf
- 1 tbsp olive oil
- 3 garlic cloves (crushed)
- 200g sour cream
- 75g shredded 3 cheese mix
- 3 green shallots (thinly sliced)

- 250g frozen spinach (thawed)
- 1 brown onion (finely chopped)
- 250g cream cheese (chopped)
- 125ml pure cream
- 35g sachet salt-reduced French onion soup mix

## Directions

Step 1. Trim the cob loaf's top by 4 cm. Remove the center of the loaf of bread, leaving a 1.5 cm thick shell. Slice or roughly chop the loaf top and inside bread into pieces. Corn and bread chunks should be placed in an air fryer.

Step 2. Spray oil on heavily. Cook for 8 minutes at 160°C while shaking the basket halfway through. the serving platter after transfer.

Step 3. In the interim, squeeze the extra liquid from the spinach using your hands.

Step 4. Heat the oil in a big frying pan with medium-high heat. Cook onion and garlic for five minutes, or until softened, stirring frequently. Low-heat setting. Add the soup mix, cream cheese, sour cream, pure cream, spinach, and shredded cheese.

Step 5. Stir thoroughly to mix. Get rid of the heat. Add two-thirds of the shallot by stirring. Use pepper to season.

Step 6. Fill bread with spinach mixture. Cover in foil entirely. the loaf in the air fryer. Cook for 15 minutes at 160C. Get rid of the foil. Cook for a further 5 minutes, or until the dip is hot and the bread is toasted.

Step 7. Serve cob loaf with toasted bread slices and the leftover onion on top.

# Ice-cream balls Air fried

**Prep : 8h 30m / Cook Time : 15 minutes / Total Time :  8h 45 mins**
**Serves  12**

## Ingredients

- 1.5L vanilla ice cream
- 3 eggs
- Caramilk sauce
- 185ml thickened cream
- 300g plain digestive biscuits (crushed)
- 1 1/2 tbsp milk
- 180g Cadbury chocolate (finely chopped)

## Directions

Step 1. A baking sheet should be chilled in the freezer for ten minutes. Baking paper is used to line the tray.

Step 2. Scoop the ice cream into 12 balls and quickly set them on the tray that has been prepared. Place for 4 hours or until solid in the freezer.

Step 3. Crush the biscuits and add them to a big shallow basin. Roll ice-cream balls in the crushed biscuits to coat, working with one at a time, and shake off extra. Back in the tray, freeze for one further hour, or until solid.

Step 4. In a bowl, whisk the milk and eggs together. Roll each ball, one at a time, in the egg mixture, then evenly coat with the remaining broken biscuits. go back to tray. Refrigerate any egg mixture that is left over.

Step 5. To double-coat, repeat coating with the remaining balls, egg mixture, and biscuit crumbs. Overnight in the freezer, until extremely stiff.

Step 6. Make the Caramilk sauce in the meantime by combining the chocolate and cream in a microwave-safe bowl. Cook for 112 minutes on high, or until chocolate is melted. until smooth, stir.

Step 7. For five minutes, preheat the air fryer at 200°C. Two ice cream balls should be placed on a small baking paper sheet. You need to be able to lift the paper with the ice-cream balls on it, but not so big that it covers the whole base of the air fryer basket. Spray some oil on.

Step 8. Place the food in the air fryer and cook for two minutes at 200 °C. Place the balls on plates for serving. Serve right away after adding Caramilk sauce.

# Beef wellington bites

**Prep : 30m / Cook Time : 12 minutes / Total Time :  43 mins**
**Serves  8**

## Ingredients

- 453g beef tenderloin (cut into 2-inch cubes)
- Olive oil spray
- 3 tbsp Dijon mustard
- 1 tbsp chopped fresh rosemary
- Salt and black pepper to taste
- 226g frozen puff pastry sheets (thawed)
- 64g chopped and cooked mushroom
- 1 egg

## Directions

Step 1. Preheat your ninja foodi air fryer at 200°C. Your air fryer's mesh rack should be greased with olive oil spray before being left aside.

Step 2. The steak bites are sprayed with olive oil spray before being salted and peppered. At 1-inch intervals, distribute the stek bites over the oiled mesh rack.

Step 3. Open the air fryer, place the mesh rack holding the beef bites in the centre and the oil drip tray on the lowest rack, then shut the door.

Step 4. To begin cooking, set the timer for 5 minutes and push the "Start/Pause" button. Depending on the desired amount of doneness, you can remove the beef either earlier or later. Remove the steak bites from the oven and place them on a plate to cool.

Step 5. Spread the steak bites across the puff pastry sheets at 2-inch intervals. Over the steak bites, sprinkle a teaspoon of Dijon mustard, some mushrooms, and rosemary. Each bite will be surrounded by a square formed by the pastry sheets.

Step 6. Beef bits are wrapped in pastries, placed on a mesh rack at 1-inch intervals, and then egg is beaten over them. Additionally, you might sprinkle them with olive oil spray.Close the air fryer's door after inserting the mesh rack containing the Beef Wellington Bites into the center rack.

Step 7. To begin cooking, set the timer for 7 minutes and push the "Start/Pause" button. Open the air fryer and take the rack out once the cooking is finished. The pastries on top should be puffy and golden brown.

Step 8. The Beef Wellington Bites should be placed on a serving plate to cool. Enjoy your classy choice!

# Christmas fruit Pudding

**Prep : 10 minutes / Cook Time : 25 minutes / Total Time :  35 mins**

### Serves  4

## Ingredients

- 85g flour
- 2 tbsp milk

- 56g sugar
- 56g soft butter

- 1 egg
- 1/2 tsp baking powder

**Fillings Ingredients**

- 128g of sliced fruit (fresh or canned)

## Directions

Step 1. Ninja foodi Air fryer should be preheated to 320°F/160°C. In a bowl, combine the topping Ingredients. For 3 minutes, beat thoroughly until mixture is soft and creamy.

Step 2. After adding the "topping" mixture to the fruit in the baking dish, level it out. Add the "filler" Ingredients.

Step 3. Bake at 320°F/160°C in an air fryer that has been prepared for 25–30 minutes, or until golden brown.

# Turkey Breast Air fried (Boneless)

### Prep : 5 minutes / Cook Time : 20 minutes / Total Time :  25 mins
### Serves  4

## Ingredients

- 1 turkey breast tenderloin (500g)
- 1/2 tsp kosher salt
- ½ tsp garlic powder
- ½ tsp paprika
- 1 tbsp olive oil
- ½ tsp onion powder
- ½ tsp thyme
- ¼ tsp ground black pepper

## Directions

Step 1. the air fryer to 360 degrees Fahrenheit. With a fresh paper towel, dry the turkey breast.

Step 2. Combine the salt, pepper, onion, garlic, thyme, and paprika in a small mixing bowl. The oil should be applied or brushed all over the turkey before the spice rub is applied to the top, bottom, and all sides of the bird.

Step 3. Place the turkey tenderloin in the air fryer basket and coat it with cooking spray or olive oil spray. The turkey should be cooked in the closed basket for 10 to 12 minutes, then turned over and cooked for 10 more minutes on the other side.

Step 4. Cook it until it reaches a temperature of 165 degrees Fahrenheit within. To determine whether the turkey is cooked through, use a meat thermometer. The turkey should be taken out of the air fryer basket once it has finished cooking and should rest for a minimum of 15 minutes before cutting and serving.

# Soft Pretzel

### Prep : 30 minutes / Cook Time : 10 minutes / Total Time :  25 mins
### Serves  8

## Dough Ingredients

- 544 all-purpose flour plus ½ cup for dusting and rolling
- 350ml of warm water around 110F
- 7g 1 packet yeast (instant or active)
- 1-2 tsp of salt
- 3 tablespoons of butter melted
- 1 tsp of sugar

### Toppings Ingredients

- 1 egg
- Everything seasoning (optional)
- 1 tbspof butter melted

## Directions

Step 1. Put warm water, butter, salt, sugar, and yeast in a large bowl. Together, stir.

Step 2. Allow the yeast to activate for ten minutes. Using a wooden spoon, add half a cup of flour at a time and whisk in the large bowl.

Step 3. The dough should be sticky after all the flour has been added.On a work surface dusted with flour, knead the dough for three to four minutes.

Step 4. When using active dry yeast, let the dough rest in a warm location for 30 minutes. If using quick yeast, omit.Create four or eight equal pieces of dough (depending on pretzel preference size).

Step 5. Each dough piece should be formed into a long rope. Shape into pretzel shapes by twisting. Prepare the egg wash while the dough is set aside.

Step 6. To make the egg wash, combine the egg and butter in a small bowl. The entire pretzel should be covered in egg wash. Do this for each pretzel. If desired, season everything.

Step 7. Spray oil on the air fryer basket. Pretzels should not be packed too tightly in the air fryer since they will expand as they cook. Cook for 12–14 minutes in the air fryer at 350°F.

# Gingerbread Cookies

**Prep : 20 minutes / Cook Time : 9 minutes / Total Time : 25 mins**
**Serves 16**

## Ingredients

- 76g butter melted
- 1 egg
- 150g brown sugar
- 140g molasses
- ¼ teaspoon ground cloves
- 1 teaspoon ground ginger
- 1 teaspoon cinnamon
- 360g flour (plus an additional 60g to be added 1 tablespoon at a time if dough is too sticky)

## Directions

Step 1. Combine sugar, molasses, egg, and melted butter. Add the cloves, ginger, and cinnamon.

Step 2. Add flour and mix. Add an extra tablespoon of flour at a time if the dough is sticky, continuing until it is no longer sticky.

Step 3. Place the dough in the freezer for ten minutes after wrapping it in plastic wrap.

Step 4. Utilizing cookie cutters, roll out the dough to a quarter-inch thickness.

In the oven, bake cookies for 12–14 minutes at 350°F (176°C), or for 8–9 minutes in an air fryer.

# Air fryer Peanut Butter Explosion Cakes

**Prep : 20 minutes / Cook Time : 9 minutes / Total Time :  25 mins**

**Serves 16**

## Ingredients

- 57g (1 stick) butter (cut into cubes, plus more for ramekins)
- 100g powdered sugar (plus more for topping)
- 1 tsp pure vanilla extract
- 34g all-purpose flour
- 4 tbsp peanut butter
- 128g chocolate chips
- 2 large eggs (plus 2 egg yolks)
- 34g unsweetened cocoa powder
- 1/2 tsp kosher salt
- 235ml water

## Directions

Step 1. Melted butter and sugars should be whisked together in a medium bowl. Whisk in the egg and vanilla after adding them. Stir in the salt, baking soda, and flour just until mixed.

Step 2. A small sheet of parchment should be placed in the air fryer's basket, leaving space around the edges to allow for airflow.

Step 3. Leaving 2" between each cookie, scoop dough onto parchment paper in batches. Press dough onto parchment to slightly flatten it.

Step 4. For 8 minutes, bake in an air fryer at 350°. The cookies will be fluffy and golden. Five minutes should pass before serving.

# Chocolate Chip Cookies

**Prep : 10 minutes / Cook Time : 35 minutes / Total Time :  45 mins**

**Serves  4-5**

## Ingredients

- 113g (1 stick) butter (melted)
- 50g granulated sugar
- 1 tsp. pure vanilla extract
- 1/2 tsp. baking soda
- 96g chocolate chips
- 55g packed brown sugar
- 1 large egg
- 204g all-purpose flour
- 1/2 tsp. kosher salt
- 43g chopped walnuts

## Directions

Step 1. Melted butter and sugars should be whisked together in a medium bowl. Whisk in the egg and vanilla after adding them. Stir in the salt, baking soda, and flour just until mixed.

Step 2. A small sheet of parchment should be placed in the air fryer's basket, leaving space around the edges to allow for airflow.

Step 3. Leaving 2" between each cookie, scoop dough onto parchment paper in batches. Press dough onto parchment to slightly flatten it.

Step 4. For 8 minutes, bake in an air fryer at 350°. The cookies will be fluffy and golden. Five minutes should pass before serving.

# Air fryer Peanut Butter Explosion Cakes

**Prep : 10 minutes / Cook Time : 35 minutes / Total Time :  45 mins**

**Serves  4**

## Ingredients

- 57g (1 stick) butter (cut into cubes, plus more for ramekins)
- 100g powdered sugar (plus more for topping)
- 1 tsp pure vanilla extract
- 34g all-purpose flour
- 4 tbsp peanut butter
- 128g chocolate chips
- 2 large eggs (plus 2 egg yolks)
- 34g unsweetened cocoa powder
- 1/2 tsp kosher salt
- 235ml water

## Directions

Step 1. 4 ramekins should be butter-greased. Melt butter and chocolate chips in a medium microwave-safe bowl in 30-second intervals until smooth. Whisk in the vanilla, egg yolks, powdered sugar, and eggs until well combined. Whisk in the flour, salt, and cocoa powder until just mixed.

Step 2. Only halfway fill the ramekins with batter, cover each with a heaping tablespoon of peanut butter. Add the remaining batter on top. Wrap foil securely around the ramekins.

Step 3. Working in batches if required, place the ramekins in the air fryer basket. Remove foil and continue cooking for an additional 6 minutes after 12 minutes at 375°.

Step 4. Ramekins should be removed from the air fryer with care. Along the edges, run a knife or offset spatula. Before serving, invert onto a dish and sprinkle with confectioner's sugar.

# Air fryer Bloomin' Apples

**Prep : 15 minutes / Cook Time : 35 minutes / Total Time :  1 hr**

**Serves 4**

## Ingredients

- Cooking spray
- 1 tbsp packed brown sugar
- 1/2 tsp ground cinnamon
- 8 chewy caramel squares
- Caramel (for drizzling)
- 4 tbsp melted butter
- 1 tbsp granulated sugar
- 4 apples
- Vanilla ice cream (Optional)

## Directions

Step 1. Combine the butter, sugars, and cinnamon in a small bowl.Each apple's top should be cut off, and the core should be removed with a melon baller (or a teaspoon).

Step 2. Cut the apple in two circles with a paring knife. Slice crosswise through the apple, cut side down, being careful not to cut through the core.

Step 3. Two caramel squares should be placed inside each apple, followed by a butter mixture brushing on top. Put sliced apples in the air fryer's basket, bake for 18 to 20 minutes at 350 degrees.

Step 4. Warm dish with ice cream and caramel drizzle.

# Brownies

**Prep : 5 minutes / Cook Time : 30 minutes / Total Time :  35 minutes**
**Serves  2**

## Ingredients

- 100g granulated sugar
- 34g all-purpose flour
- Pinch kosher salt
- 1 large egg
- 45g cocoa powder
- 1/4 tsp baking powder
- 57g butter (melted)

## Directions

Step 1. Cooking spray should be used to grease a 6" round cake pan before combining sugar, cocoa powder, flour, baking soda, and salt in a medium basin.

Step 2. Melted butter and egg are whisked together in a small bowl before being added to the dry Ingredients and mixed.

Step 3. Transfer brownie batter to the prepared cake pan, smooth the surface, and cook in the air fryer at 350° for 16 to 18 minutes.

# Air fryer Cannoli

**Prep : 10 minutes / Cook Time : 10 minutes / Total Time :  3 hrs**
**Yields 20**

## Ingredients
**FILLING:**
- 1 (453g) container ricotta
- 100g powdered sugar (divided)
- 1 tsp pure vanilla extract
- 1/4 tsp kosher salt
- 170g mascarpone cheese
- 255g heavy cream
- 1 tsp orange zest
- 64g mini chocolate chips (garnish

**SHELLS:**
- 275g all-purpose flour, plus more for surface
- 1 tsp kosher salt
- 4 tbsp cold butter (cubes)
- 1 large egg
- 50g granulated sugar
- 1/2 tsp cinnamon
- 6 tbsp white wine
- 1 egg white (brushing)

## Directions

**FILLING:**

Step 1. Place a fine mesh strainer over a big basin to drain the ricotta. Let the food drip in the refrigerator for up to overnight.

Step 2. Use a hand mixer to whisk 1/4 cup powdered sugar and heavy cream in a big bowl until stiff peaks form.

Step 3. Ricotta, mascarpone, the remaining 1/4 cup powdered sugar, vanilla, orange zest, and salt should all be combined in a different big bowl.

Step 4. Add whipped cream and fold. Refrigerate for at least an hour before filling cannoli.

**Shells :**

Step 1. Mix the flour, sugar, salt, and cinnamon in a sizable bowl. Using your hands or a pastry cutter, blend the butter into the flour mixture until pea-sized.

Step 2. Mix until a dough forms after adding the wine and egg. For the dough to come together, knead it in the bowl a few times. Pat into a circle, cover with plastic wrap, and chill for at least one hour and maybe overnight.

Step 3. Divide the dough in half and place on a lightly dusted surface. One side is rolled out to be 1/8" thick. To cut out dough, use a 4" round cookie cutter.

Step 4. Use the leftover dough to repeat. Reroll leftover bits to make a couple more circles.

Step 5. Egg white should be brushed where the dough will meet to glue it together. Wrap dough around cannoli molds.

**Start Air frying**

Step 1. Molds should be placed in the air fryer basket in batches and cooked for 12 minutes at 350° or until golden.

Step 2. Gently twist the shells away from the molds after they are cool enough to handle or when using a dish towel to hold them.

Step 3. Fill a pastry bag with the filling and attach an open star tip. Fill shells with filling and then roll the ends in small chocolate chips.

# Air fryer Crustless Cheesecake

**Prep : 10 minutes / Cook Time : 10 minutes / Total Time :  20 minutes**
**Serving 2**

## Ingredients

• 453g cream cheese
• 2 eggs
• 1/2 tsp lemon juice

• 150g zero calorie sweetener
• 1 tsp vanilla extract
• 2 tbsp sour cream

## Directions

Step 1. Set the air fryer's temperature to 350 degrees. Blend the eggs, sweetener, vanilla, and lemon juice until thoroughly combined. Blend in the sour cream and cream cheese until smooth and lump-free. It will become creamier the more you whip it.

Step 2. Fill two 4-inch springform pans with batter, and bake for 8 to 10 minutes, or until firm.

Step 3. Allow the springform pan to completely cool. Place in the fridge for at least two to three hours. Enjoy!

# Air fryer Crustless Cheesecake

**Prep : 10 minutes / Cook Time : 10 minutes / Total Time : 20 minutes**
**Serving 4**

## Ingredients

- 1.5 Tbsp Self Rising Flour
- 100g Unsalted Butter
- 2 Eggs
- 3.5 tbsp Baker's Sugar (Not Powdered)
- 100g Dark Chocolate (Pieces or Chopped)

## Directions

Step 1. Grease and flour four regular oven-safe ramekins. Preheat your air fryer to 375°F. Melt butter and dark chocolate together in a microwave-safe bowl on level 7 for three minutes while stirring. When done, remove from microwave and whisk until smooth.

Step 2. Eggs and sugar should be whisked or beat until light and foamy. Add the melted chocolate to the egg mixture. Add flour and mix. To evenly incorporate everything, use a spatula.

Step 3. Bake the cake mixture in the prepared air fryer at 375F for 10 minutes, filling the ramekins about 3/4 full.

Step 4. Take out of the air fryer, then let cool in the ramekin for two minutes. Turn the ramekins carefully upside down onto the serving dish while loosening the edges by tapping the bottom with a butter knife.

Step 5. Cake should easily pop out of the ramekin and have a dark, gooey center. Enjoy warm or with a raspberry drizzle, a-la-mode.

# Air fryer Banana Pancake Dippers

**Prep : 10 minutes / Cook Time : 10 minutes / Total Time : 20 minutes**
**Serving 4**

## Ingredients

- 3 bananas (halved and sliced lengthwise)
- Melted chocolate ( Optional)
- 1 tbsp butter

**Batter**

- 204g all-purpose flour
- 2 tbsp packed brown sugar
- 177ml whole milk
- 2 large eggs
- 1 tbsp baking powder
- 1 tsp kosher salt
- 170g sour cream
- 1 tsp pure vanilla extract

## Directions

Step 1. Mix the flour, baking soda, brown sugar, and salt in a big bowl. Whisk the milk, sour cream, and eggs in a separate bowl before adding each egg one at a time. Add vanilla and stir. With a wooden spoon, mix the dry Ingredients after adding the wet ones.

Step 2. Cooking spray should be used to oil and parchment paper the air fryer basket. Put bananas on parchment paper in a single layer after dipping them in pancake batter in batches.

Step 3. 16 minutes of cooking @ 350° until golden. For dipping, serve with melted chocolate.

# Fried oreos

**Prep : 10 minutes / Cook Time : 4 minutes / Total Time :  14 minutes**
**Serving 9**

## Ingredients

• 9 oreo cookies

• 1 crescent sheet roll

## Directions

Step 1. Spread the pop crescent out on the table. Line up and cut 9 equal squares with a knife.

Step 2. Grab nine cookies, then enclose them in those squares. Set air fryer to 360 degrees of heat.

Step 3. Cook wrapped cookies in a single layer for 4 minutes, stirring and rotating once. If desired, garnish with cinnamon or powdered sugar.

# Chocolate Cake

**Prep : 10 minutes / Cook Time : 25 minutes / Total Time :  35 minutes**
**Serving 4**

## Ingredients

• 3 eggs

• 136g flour

• 8 tablespoons butter (room temperature)

• 1 teaspoon baking powder

• 2 teaspoons vanilla extract

**FROSTING**

• 400g icing powdered sugar

• 2 tablespoons cocoa powder

• ⅛ teaspoon salt

• 85g sour cream

• 134g sugar

• 45g cocoa powder

• ½ teaspoon baking soda

• 8 tablespoons butter (room temperature)

• 2 tablespoons heavy cream

## Directions

Step 1. Set your air fryer to 320°F before using. On low speed, use a hand mixer to combine the cake Ingredients.

Step 2. In the air fryer's oven attachment, which has been coated with non-stick spray, pour the cake batter.

Slide the object into the air fryer's basket. clock to 25 minutes.

Step 3. Use a toothpick to check whether the cake is done once the timer goes off. Cook for an extra

5 minutes if the food does not spring back when touched.On a wire rack, cool the cake. After your cake has cooled, frost it.

Step 4. FROSTING: On low speed, beat the frosting Ingredients until thoroughly combined.

Step 5. Decorate the cooled cake with frosting. Slice, then dish.

# Air fryer Sugar Orange donut

**Prep : 20 minutes / Cook Time : 15 minutes / Total Time :  35 minutes**
**Yields 15**

## Ingredients

• 1 sheet puff pastry (500g) (thawed)
• Melted butter as needed
• Sugar mixture
• ¼ cup sugar
• 1 tsp finely grated orange zest
• ¼ tsp ground cardamom

## Directions

Step 1.Prepare sugar mixture. Puff pastry should be unfolded, then cut into four strips that are each an even 2 14 inches across, with a 1 12 inch bias on each. apart (to construct parallelograms) (to make parallelograms). Make holes in the dough with a fork.

Step 3. Orange-Cardamom Sugar: In bowl, using fingers, combine sugar,  orange zest and ground cardamom until mixture reaches consistency of brown sugar. Set aside.

Step 2. Batch-air-fry at 350°F for about 3 minutes each side, flipping once, or until golden brown. Toss immediately with sugar mixture, using butter to help it stick if required. Serve and enjoy.

Printed in Great Britain
by Amazon

15968023R00050